GOLDEN COCOON

An autobiographical experience of two elderly people who firmly believed that a Continuing Care Retirement Community was the answer to growing old with dignity.

GOLDEN COCOON

Virginia K. Lindstrom

and

Carl A. Lindstrom

 RAGGED EDGE PRESS

This Ragged Edge Press publication
was printed by
Beidel Printing House, Inc.
63 West Burd Street
Shippensburg, PA 17257 USA

This book was printed on permanent acid-free paper.

To protect those involved in this story, all names except those of the authors and governmental agency respondents have been changed.

This book is sold with the understanding that neither the author nor the publisher is engaged in rendering legal or professional advice.

For a complete list of available publications
please write
Ragged Edge Press
Division of White Mane Publishing Company, Inc.
P.O. Box 152
Shippensburg, PA 17257 USA

Library of Congress Cataloging-in-Publication Data

Lindstrom, Virginia, 1918-
    Golden Cocoon / by Virginia K. & Carl A. Lindstrom.
        p.   cm.
    ISBN 0-942597-88-5 (hard : alk. paper) : $19.95
    1. Life care communities--United States--Case Studies.   2. Life
care communities--United States--Evaluation.   I. Lindstrom, Carl
A., 1918-   . II. Title.
HV1454.2.U5L56 1995
362.1'6'0973--dc20   95-33330
                                                                  CIP

*T*his book is dedicated to Dorothy Easterday, my sister, my friend, whose dedication to Mother when she was a patient in the Baptist Nursing Home inspired me to volunteer in Ashley House, Elm Grove's skilled nursing facility. There I learned the double meaning of the Admissions Director's plaque, "When you need it, it's too late."

Virginia K. Lindstrom

CONTENTS

FOREWORD

Many publications extol Continuing Care Retirement Communities as places in which the elderly may live out their lives with dignity. Such publications also provide guidance in tailoring a prospective resident to a Community of his choice. *Golden Cocoon* does neither. Rather than titillating the prospective resident with descriptions of fun-and-games and leisure, of the lounges and dining rooms, of swimming pools and putting greens, of living accommodations and health care, *Golden Cocoon* offers an insight into "the other side of the coin."

The "other side of the coin" is the dark side of a Continuing Care Retirement Community. Here are found those patients with dementia, the deaf, and the blind; those patients who are weak, fatigued, and depressed; and those physically disabled by stroke, Parkinson's disease, or Alzheimer's disease—all infirm and residing in the Community's long-term care facility. Among such residents are those who are alone with no guardian or surrogate to oversee their welfare—those who are forgotten and who may be treated with indifference by the Community and its staff.

Golden Cocoon focuses on the rights and well-being of the elderly helpless, incompetent, and incapacitated patients in Continuing Care Retirement Communities, and the rights of volunteers who, as independent residents of the Community, may assist them. The experiences of the authors when they dared to defend and claim their rights and those of all independent residents and helpless patients in Continuing Care Retirement Communities in the Commonwealth of Pennsylvania will alert the prospective resident to the fact that there is much more than fun-and-games to explore.

The events in *Golden Cocoon* are true. However, the name of the Continuing Care Retirement Community, Elm Grove, is fictional as are the names of all persons except the authors' and governmental agency respondents.

INTRODUCTION

If you, as an aging person, are concerned about your well-being, if, or when, you may be unable to care for yourself; if you are doubly concerned because there is no one to assist you and you don't choose to be a burden on family, friends, or the government, a Continuing Care Retirement Community (CCRC) with a continuum of care may be your Shangri La. From the day of entry to the CCRC you should be able to live independently as you would in your own home and when physical or mental abilities diminish, there should be others to attend and serve you for the rest of your life. Living quarters, housekeeping, household maintenance, and food service should be provided. Breakfast, lunch, and dinner may be served in a formal dining room or cozy coffee shop on the premises. Transportation by bus or van to shopping malls, grocery stores, and for medical or dental appointments will make owning an automobile an option. On and off campus there should be social events, arts and crafts, entertainment, and church services for mental stimulation. Tonsorial attention, a library, a gift shop, and perhaps a branch bank and post office may be added conveniences. Reinforced by the socialized medical cost-and-payment structure of the CCRC you should have assurance of lifetime health care. With that come personal care where nurses and aides provide assistance in bathing, dressing, taking medications, and such if need arises; and skilled nursing care during a period of convalescence, or if you are permanently non-ambulatory, bedridden, or incompetent. Select such a CCRC and you will be in a "golden cocoon"—you may even be a resident of Elm Grove.

All CCRCs with a continuum of care are alike in that they promise care for life, but there are differences among them in how they accomplish that goal. There are variations in health care plans; in the availability of special-care facilities on-campus, such as personal and skilled nursing care; in provision of catered services such as housekeeping, household maintenance and food; in accommodations offered and accompanying amenities; in entrance fees and plans for refunds; in on-going costs after entrance; in minimum age requirements and wellness standards for admission as a resident; in plans for assurance of lifetime health care itself; in ownership or sponsorship; in management; in the acquisition of income as for-profit or not-for-profit; and more.

Hundreds of CCRCs have already been built in the United States, and, with our aging population, their number increases yearly. Thousands of people are moving to, thinking of moving to, or investigating CCRCs as the best solution to the problems that age and infirmity present.

The CCRCs, whether for-profit or not-for-profit, conduct themselves as businesses and supposedly are under governmental regulations which vary according to location. Some CCRCs are commercially owned and operated; others are owned or sponsored by religious organizations, community-spirited coalitions, or by fraternal orders, among others. Management may be internal or contractual. If the CCRC is sponsored by an organized religious group and one is not of that persuasion, acceptance as a resident may not be entirely benevolent, for state and federal laws forbid discrimination. Such admissions, however, help keep the CCRC solvent and without such help it probably couldn't survive.

Perhaps you have been impressed by the numerous glossy and colorful brochures which picture these Communities as exotic islands of paradise, sometimes putting the real islands to shame. One wonders if all these brochures, cassettes, and newspaper advertisements were prepared by the same PR firm since all extol similar values and standards—independence, security, new opportunities, full continuum of care, definitely non-institutionalization, high-quality health care programs, treatment of individuals as valued persons with dignity and respect, camaraderie, and friendliness. They paint graphic pictures of their amenities—the landscaping, the lounges, the library, the dining room, beauty and barber shops, and certainly the apartments. They recite their activities—arts and crafts, on-campus entertainment, "things to do," and in a very specific way they carry the same message—"Come live with us!"

But none of the brochures, cassettes, tapes, or pamphlets are able to present the demeanor and posture of the administration, the staff, yes, and even the residents, which only an on-site daily contact may reveal; how the CCRC may subtly invade one's privacy as it monitors behavior daily, and how a dossier, so compiled, may be abused; how the administration can dictate health care destiny, and how it may discipline and even evict a resident who has absolutely no recourse under the signed agreement. None will explicitly spell out the CCRC's socialized cost-and-payment structure to enable a prospective resident to decide if he or she is willing to accept such a system; or reveal the on-going bills in addition to the maintenance fee which may be presented each month. And many of the brochures do not expand on the probable financial loss if one voluntarily vacates the CCRC, is evicted, or dies.

"Taking care of you" in the advertisements never hints at how a CCRC's incapacitated elderly—those vulnerable individuals in its midst—may be denied advocacy by the administration through threats, intimidation, and retaliation against the advocate in order to quash complaints and, thereby, protect the Community's image. The advertisements will not reveal the weakness and fragility of a resident's rights—which, supposedly supported by governmental statute, CCRC policies, and contractual agreement—may be abrogated at will by the administration once the resident enters the CCRC.

The advertisements only extol. They do not—they would not—they could not—warn of anything negative which a resident might encounter.

When searching for a Continuing Care Retirement Community which is just right for you, keep in mind that there are two aspects of a CCRC: the physical plant, that is, the superstructure; and the human plant, that is, the infrastructure. The former is quite visible—the landscaping, the lounge, the dining room—the up-front part. It is the latter, composed of the administration, the staff, and even the residents, which is always vague and indefinite, but it is here where your faith and trust must be placed.

An administrator of a Delaware River Valley Continuing Care Retirement Community testified when his Community was in the process of accreditation, "From what we consider to be a position of strength, the Board can plan in a positive way for future leadership and involvement, always recognizing that *trust* among all components of the Community—Board, residents, staff—is what holds it together." In one's search for a Continuing Care Retirement Community to call home, he may arm himself with authoritative guidelines, with careful planning and logic reinforced by experiences as he goes along, but when he makes a selection it will only be on faith and trust that he commits his destiny to the administration and staff—yes, even to the residents.

Faith and trust! There is so much about the Community selected as a home for the remainder of one's life that will not surface until after admission. Consider carefully the "cocoon" waiting out there which you might ultimately select, for it well might disintegrate when once you've settled in.

May *Golden Cocoon* help in your evaluation.

The announcement in the *Elm Grove Bulletin* read:

"The featured speaker at the September Forum will be Ms. Dorothy Anderson, Director of the Area Agency on Aging in our County. She will deal with the many problems related to an increasingly older population in the United States, the specific problems faced by older people (and also their children in many cases), and outline the State and County services available to help families. The talk will be given on Tuesday, September 25, 1990 at 7:00 P.M. in Elm Hall. The County Area Agency on Aging which Ms. Anderson directs is one of fifty-two in the Commonwealth of Pennsylvania and is responsible for planning, funding, coordinating, and delivering a wide range of programs. Ms. Anderson has worked for our County since 1960 and has pioneered the development of many of the programs she now administers."

Elm Hall was filled the evening of September 25, 1990 with those Elm Grove residents who were curious about the Area Agency on Aging. The address, however, had little to do with the care of the frail and elderly at Elm Grove. Instead, it spelled out the broad goal of the Department of Adult Services which was "to develop comprehensive services to assist older people to remain independent and prevent premature institutionalization." The priorities of the Department, as laid out by Ms. Anderson, are "the frail elderly, over 75 with chronic disabilities who are living alone and with low income; and minorities." This scarcely applied to the residents of Elm Grove.

The audience was told that services for the aging are financed under federal, state, and county statutes that require the Area Agency on Aging to investigate all reports of incapacitated elderly age 60 and older at imminent risk of abuse to ensure that services necessary for the health, safety, and welfare of these vulnerable individuals are provided 24-hours a day, seven days a week, and that a long-term care ombudsman program receives, investigates, and verifies complaints about nursing homes, personal care boarding homes and long-term care services in the County.

But Ms. Anderson pointed out that Elm Grove people, in their "golden cocoon" didn't have to worry about these things. I had heard Elm Grove referred to as "The Cadillac" or "The Rolls Royce" of Continuing Care Retirement Communities but this was the first time I had heard it called a "golden cocoon". Surely Ms. Anderson was aware of the old cliche, "All that glitters is not gold!" Certainly this glittering "cocoon", Elm Grove, was not gold. For less than one week prior to this address, I had learned that this chrysalis was really brass with an iron fist hidden inside. I had been pounded by that fist for over an hour and fifteen minutes after being summoned to the office of the administrator and his associate. During that inquisition I learned that Elm Grove's administration was not as concerned about its incapacitated elderly at imminent risk of abuse as it was about Elm Grove's reputation— that at Elm Grove anyone attempting to advocate on behalf of vulnerable individuals in their midst or complain about their treatment would be threatened with legal action, intimidated, belittled, and retaliated against, for "Elm Grove has a good reputation across the United States and would not allow anyone to damage that image!"

Following that encounter it wasn't a beautiful butterfly but rather an ugly truth that emerged from Carl's and my "golden cocoon".

"FAILURE TO PROVIDE
THE CARE AND TREATMENT NECESSARY
TO MAINTAIN THE WELFARE
OF THOSE WHO DEPEND ON THAT CARE
IS EVERY BIT AS DANGEROUS AND HARMFUL
AS INTENTIONAL ASSAULTIVE BEHAVIOR."

*NATIONAL ASSOCIATION
OF ATTORNEYS GENERAL*

CHAPTER I

"YOU SHOULD HAVE LOOKED AT JUST ONE MORE!"

My husband, Carl, and I moved to Elm Grove during the second week of December 1989. Thereafter, each night at dinner when we shared a table with some member of the welcoming committee whose goal it was to make us feel at home, we were asked the same question over and over again: "We've been told you inspected more than two dozen Continuing Care Retirement Communities. What made you choose Elm Grove? What made you come here?" It was almost as though they were pleading for an explanation that would satisfy their being here—that they wanted assurance that they hadn't made a mistake and that Elm Grove really was the best. But it wasn't until the following year, September 19, in the office of the administrator of Elm Grove and his associate, when that question was repeated one final time, that I knew Carl and I had made a mistake in coming to Elm Grove, when, with strident voice oozing hostility the associate lashed out at me with, "Mrs. Lindstrom, why did you come to Elm Grove? What do you like about it here?"

Yes, we had made a mistake—the most devastating mistake of our 70 plus years—but it wasn't the result of any impetuous action. Carl and I had begun our quest for a Life Care Community, as a Continuing Care Retirement Community was called originally, many years before adding our name to Elm Grove's waiting list of prospective residents. We had had a difficult time finding satisfactory nursing home care for my mother and Carl's mother when they needed it. In Sun City, Arizona, an active retirement/resort community where we had lived for sixteen years, we had mothered a number of similar older couples in our neighborhood, who, although they had enjoyed the active part of their retirement years, had advanced through age to the point where they could no longer care for themselves. This was not going to happen to us! Before arriving at that state in our lives we were determined to find accommodations in a caring, attractive, well-maintained, well-managed and highly respected Life Care Community. It must have three levels of care—independent living; assisted living, sometimes called personal care, which we considered the most necessary; and skilled nursing care, which, hopefully, we would never need as a permanent inpatient since only a small percentage of older persons end their lives that way.

We had been introduced to Life Care Communities through a United States Public Health Service nurse who was anticipating the day when she might not be able to care for herself. She had been checking some Pacific Homes Communities sponsored by the United Methodist Church.

When we were assigned to Phoenix we discovered that there was a Pacific Homes Community at the foot of Squaw Peak. One Sunday afternoon it had open house to which the surrounding metropolis was invited and my husband and I made a visit. This was a rewarding two hours, for, during that time, we learned that if we paid the onetime, lump-sum fee for entrance (this being called the entrance fee) to a two-bedroom/two-bath unit for both of us, upgraded and decorated that unit as we would our own home, when one of us died the other had to give up that unit immediately for a one-bedroom/one-bath unit because one person was not allowed to occupy a two-bedroom/two-bath unit.

However, a spinster doctor acquaintance of ours was given a two-bedroom/two-bath unit there not long after this visit and we subsequently learned, as we progressed in our search, that money undoubtedly could accomplish many things.

We did take time that Sunday afternoon to read the bulletin boards, a must-do when one visits any Community. On one board, in plain view of the invited visitors, was a note signed by a number of the residents asking if the kitchen wouldn't clean the orange juice machine to rid the beverage of its foul taste.

The Squaw Peak complex was not pursued further.

On a trip to Southern California we merely drove by Communities which we had identified on our own, or which had been brought to our attention by acquaintances, when a drive-by was enough. If there were no pride in maintaining the visible part of the structure, we had no interest in calling such places home. This final home of ours should be one we would be proud to invite our friends to visit.

However, on a trip to Hawaii, as we drove by a Pacific Homes Community we were impressed by what we saw on the outside and decided that we should make an appointment with the administrator of this Kaneohe complex for a visit. We now knew, though, that a group of residents at some Pacific Homes Communities who had been promised life care, contractually, at a restricted increase in their monthly maintenance fee—a fee paid by each resident for basic services provided by the Community—had brought suit against Pacific Homes and the United Methodist Church, Pacific Homes' sponsor. Pacific Homes, finding itself in a financial bind, was attempting to abrogate the contract. The suit was bitter; CBS's *60 Minutes* had documented it on national TV.

The Kaneohe Community sat high on a hill overlooking the ocean. The view was spectacular, the landscaping lush and gorgeous—the apartment we were shown, seedy.

We were invited to stay for lunch for which we insisted on paying and we found it spartan to say the least—an ungarnished egg salad sandwich, a cup of broth, and a cookie. We were positive that the dining room had been an elegant room in days long passed done in yellow and green, with magnificent views of the ocean below through expansive windows. But this room, too, was now badly in need of refurbishing.

While discussing admission with the administrator, there was no mention of monetary or legal problems but we were offered a lease. This became an important part of our education. Henceforth, we would be wary of Communities which had numerous vacancies—Communities which would offer leases so as to fill their living units when previously entrance fees had been required. Of course, such practices would help defray expenses, for monthly maintenance fees billed to the residents must be adjusted periodically to meet the cost of operating the Community, and empty units can create financial havoc.

Our interest in Pacific Homes was completely dispelled by this trip to Hawaii.

On subsequent trips to California we stopped briefly at a high-rise complex in the heart of San Francisco, sedate and beautiful but indifferent to our visit. At that particular time this facility would take applications only from males and couples; they were not interested in a population that was predominately female. In Oakland we found a Community which was crowded on a tiny parcel of land across the street from a city park. Residents at lunch informed us that it wasn't safe to walk in that park at any time. Walking was important and we had no intention of becoming a prisoner in a small apartment.

Santa Barbara, with its great climate and its lovely old Mission, must certainly be a good place to live. There, high on a bluff overlooking the Pacific, we found The Cliffs. The apartments were spacious and elegant—all strung out along the Pacific. The unit we were shown had a magnificent view of the Mission from the living room window. A little conveyance, much like a string of tiny golf carts, went 'round the area picking up residents to take them to lunch and dinner. Here was a point to make note of—we were ambulatory now, walking was fun, we could appreciate a hike to the dining room and back. This would be great for the digestion. But thinking ahead five years or more—a broken hip? arthritic knees? a faltering heart? We must remember to take into account the distance to the dining room, the lounge, the doctor's office. How would we manage this in years to come?

Admission age at The Cliffs was low as compared with other Communities we had visited. Although we were barely 55 we could have acquired that lovely apartment we were shown with its great view and lush carpeting. We ate lunch that noon with a couple in their early 60's who told us that their friends had scoffed at their moving to a "nursing home" so soon, but they wanted to be able to enjoy the amenities of the area before they got too old to do so. This, too, was our philosophy.

The dining room, on the second floor of a circular building, was beautiful, tastefully furnished, with a majestic view of the ocean. From the window we could see a large outdoor swimming pool on the grounds which our hosts professed to enjoy; and they also pointed out their tennis court, both of which had an appeal to us until we learned they were shared with a local athletic club. "This sharing, you know, helps to keep down our monthly expenses!" True, but would the courts and pool be available for those residents who wanted to use them or would the club have priority?

Here, too, we encountered another item that was high on our list of must-haves. We didn't find the three levels of care in separated facilities which we knew a Life Care Community should have. We wanted a home where those who require only a little help daily in dressing, bathing, taking medicines and other simple, but necessary, personal needs, would not be lodged among skilled nursing care inpatients who are totally incapable of taking care of themselves. So, on up the West Coast we proceeded.

It was a lovely summer afternoon when we found our way to a Community in Seattle in close proximity to the Seattle Cultural Center. There are numerous opportunities for entertainment in Seattle with its many fine restaurants, modern shopping centers, the Cultural Center itself, but what about the year-round climate? How does the aging resident handle black ice or snowy pavements? So after visiting more than a dozen Communities from San Diego to Seattle, we concluded the Life Care Communities on the Pacific Coast were not for us.

Next we explored the Rocky Mountain states starting in Santa Fe, New Mexico. The Community we visited there was a reclaimed motel—nothing elegant and nothing pleasing about it.

In Colorado Springs we rejected a Community which had been established in a depressed area. Small, old, vacant and run-down houses were clustered around the Community's multi-storied building. This added a new dimension to our list of things to be aware of. The adjoining neighborhoods must be more thoroughly investigated.

"Golden Doors" and "Happy Endings" and homes with names that denoted age and senility were not for us. Like Helen Hayes, we did not mind growing old for it's part of living, but such names are demeaning. Surely anyone who would choose a name like this for his Community would have a condescending attitude. We wanted to be treated with the dignity our years had bought.

In Boulder City we noted the inaccessibility of a very nicely kept facility. It was way out on the prairie, so to speak. There would certainly come a day when we could no longer drive and I could, in no way, visualize our sitting on a rocker on the veranda of that home even if Father Time had started his count down.

While we were looking into and around Life Care Communities in the West, we also, during trips to the East, found time to see what was offered there. South along the Gulf Coast and up the Atlantic side of Florida provided some very interesting and educational experiences.

An architecturally elegant high-rise, church-sponsored Community on the Gulf had all the amenities we deemed necessary, but we were told, when we asked to see their skilled nursing care section, that "You can go into the skilled nursing care area only if you live here!" Wouldn't that be too late to find patients lying on pallets of straw or chained to their beds or sore-ridden lying in their own feces? At the same complex, when I asked if we could have lunch in their dining room, for which we were expecting to pay, that same marketing agent said, "We don't allow people to come in off the street to our dining room." Having written to this Life Care Community from Sun City, Arizona, and having been granted an appointment at a specific time on a specified date we didn't feel as though we were "coming in off the street". Imagine living with such an arrogant administration for ten or twenty more years!

In the same general area we visited a most attractive Community—bright and gay in its decor but with sanitary waste from the complex being discharged into the ground, seeping out, and trickling down the cliff into the Gulf below. Proper waste disposal now is very necessary else in coming years the residents will be saddled with the cost of government-mandated sewage disposal facilities.

"Beauty is everywhere" advertised the nicely maintained Community in southwest Florida. And indeed it was! We spent almost a week in a motel built on their grounds which we presumed had been placed there to house winter visitors to their church activities and conferences. This was a thoughtfully planned village with its own marina, indoor and outdoor pools, saunas, well-conceived exercise room, light and well-furnished craft rooms, small grocery store, coffee shop, adequate library and immaculate landscaping. The administrator was courteous and willing to please. He offered accommodations in both garden and multi-storied apartments. Empty units, and there were many, would be decorated to suit the occupant. We were most impressed with their skilled nursing care facility which had a large, screened sun porch where elderly patients had been wheeled to look over the picture-book landscape. We drank in the beauty of a huge garden of tropical plants and trees surrounding a lagoon. Birds and butterflies hovered over hibiscus flowers of red, pink, white, and yellow. Soft music played in the background and I thought, "Even if these elderly folks aren't aware of what's going on around them the beauty of this well-kept paradise must be more than soothing."

But, to us, all was less than perfect in this Garden of Eden. True, it was a church-sponsored Community and wherever we went, along the paths lined with flowers, to the dining room, to the craft rooms, we were confronted constantly by well-meaning pious souls who kept demanding whether or not we had been "born again". This, after a week, got old. How irritating in a couple of years.

And fortunate were we that we weren't visiting during a hurricane that might be headed toward the Gulf side of the peninsula. For the village was built on land reclaimed from the sea. A narrow road led from the village to the main highway. What about evacuation in case of a devastating storm?

How well do I remember the high-pressure salesman in the Palisades area. "We'll put two apartments together for you on the top floor to make a spacious penthouse for you. No children? There's no point in your dying with any money left. Enjoy it while you can!" And when he learned that we thoroughly enjoyed square dancing he led us to a cozy atrium bordered by tropical plants and declared, "There! We'll let you use this area for your square dances when you move in!"

As obliging as this agent had been, we found the sales representative in Orlando just the opposite. He bristled at my questions—and by now I had a notebook full—and with raised eyebrows and sarcastic voice he said, "Well, these communities aren't for everyone and you obviously would be happier somewhere else!" This wasn't the first time we felt such arrogance and it certainly wouldn't be the last. But, I'm sure as I write this, that it is far better to encounter arrogance before choosing a Community than to face it after moving in.

It was also in the Orlando area where we found a Community unique in its concept. This complex consisted of a number of very nice, spacious, well-designed duplexes and a high-rise closeby consisting of single rooms and baths which was the personal care and skilled nursing care facility. One purchased a side of a duplex, and each year for ten years he used up a prorated part of his purchase price. If, along the way, he needed personal care or skilled nursing care as a permanent inpatient, that part of the purchase price of the duplex remaining could be used to help pay the current entrance fee for accommodation in the high-rise. Entrance fees for rooms in the high-rise escalated annually with the cost of living but the original purchase price for the duplex remained the same for the purchaser. If one believes actuarial statistics, such an arrangement might be satisfactory if one were over eighty years of age when he moved into the duplex but if he purchased a duplex at age sixty-five or so, surely one should not assume that there would be any funds left from the original price paid for the duplex to apply to a room in the personal care or skilled nursing care section in the high-rise when such a need might become necessary.

Along the coastal area of Virginia we came upon a high-rise, all units of which had a view of the ocean. When we asked if the Community had three levels of care, we were told there was no personal care, which of the three we felt was most important. The administrator said most kindly, "In case of such a need we will find an aide for you." This was a very nice gesture but a costly added expense to the hefty monthly maintenance fee. When we inquired about transportation to doctors' offices, for shopping sprees and other needed outings, we were told that the city bus stopped right at the door so there was no need for a Community van. Great! But what happens if in future years with city budget strained to the limit such bus service is curtailed or eliminated? What if there is no taxi service? Is one to impose on younger residents with driving privileges to provide transportation? Our aversion to this idea was our reason for leaving Sun City.

Each time we visited a Community someone on the staff or some resident with whom we chatted would tell us about another place to add to our list of must-sees. And thus, eventually, we found ourselves in the Philadelphia area.

Glenside—very attractive and well designed—was crowded on small acreage. There were no walks or paths; there was nothing inside or out which would provide for physical exercise. A YMCA a few miles down the street provided a place for workouts but that held little interest for us. So, although our gracious dinner hostess glorified her lovely apartment and Glenside, although there was a very nice dining room which served delicious and attractive foods, and although we would have the amenities of a metropolis at our doorstep we decided to leave Glenside to others. However, it was during our visit here that we were introduced to other Communities in the Delaware River Valley.

The administrator at Homestead, the first of a religious order of Communities we visited, was exceedingly courteous. When I had finished asking questions about life at Homestead, he informed me that I had neglected to ask a very important question—were the members of the Board of Directors paid? And sure enough, at our very next stop when I asked that question, I discovered that they were. Surely such an item would add to a Community's expenses and residents' bills.

Let me explain at this point that all of these establishments were not investigated by my husband and me in just a short time. This process was over a number of years and each and every visit had added something to our general knowledge.

In the meantime we met a Sun City couple, about our age, on a similar quest. Every time one of us would find a new Community we'd report back to the other describing the location, the accommodations, the amenities, the attitude of the administration, and the health care. We all noticed that, seemingly, the most important activity of the day in every Community was the dinner hour. Perhaps it's because most elderly people yearn for companionship, for something to highlight the day. At any rate, in best bib-and-tucker, they would line up early outside the dining area waiting for the doors to open. So we and our friends added to our prerequisites the facts that the dining room should be ultra-attractive, the residents should be allowed to choose their dining companions, the food should be of superior quality, and the plates graciously and attractively served.

In comparing notes with our Sun City friends, Pauline shared a funny experience. She told about eating lunch in a dining room where the residents sat at long tables. A waitress with a basket of over-ripe bananas stood at the end of the table and passed the brown, soft bananas down the line from one resident to another. Pauline said, "I felt just like a monkey in a zoo!" After laughing about this she and I decided that, henceforth, a dining room would have to pass the 'banana test'. Whether at noon or at the dinner hour during our visits we'd ask for a banana for dessert. The way it was served would tell us much about the Community's pride in their kitchen and service. Shortly after, Carl and I had occasion to eat in The Meadows' dining room and they more than passed the test. How did I want the banana? Sliced? With milk, cream, or ice-cream? When it arrived, and I had merely asked that it be sliced, it was attractively served in a glass compote on a glass dish. Indeed, these were people who did strive for excellence, albeit this was just the 'banana test'.

During the next two years Carl and I visited numerous Communities in the Delaware River Valley, the Lehigh River Valley, and in the southeastern and south central regions of Pennsylvania. And along the way we found Elm Grove which had opened in the spring of 1980, although it was not until 1982 that we visited for the first time. Shortly thereafter, Carl and I decided that, as a Continuing Care Retirement Community, Elm Grove was as nearly perfect as any we would find.

The admissions director told us that Elm Grove had a waiting list of prospective residents—it would be at least two to two and one-half years before we could enter which suited us perfectly. The admission age was sixty-five and we were sixty-three. We, like the couple with whom we had dined at The Cliffs in Santa Barbara, were going to enter our Community early. Carl and I had lived in the West for twenty years and had roamed the roads and byways of all the western states, had toured Hawaii, Alaska, and southwestern Canada a number of times. But, although he and I were born and reared in Pennsylvania, we had left Pittsburgh forty-five years ago and the eastern part of Pennsylvania, New York, New England, and southeastern Canada were beckoning. We had much to explore while we could still navigate on our own. The desire to navigate brought us to another reason for entering Elm Grove early. We understood that one had to be ambulatory and in good health to be admitted. During our years in Sun City we had watched the physical and mental deterioration of our neighbors and acquaintances after age seventy, and the admissions director's sign on her office wall at Elm Grove which read, "When you need it, it's too late", sounded ominous. We were ready to settle in. We put our name on Elm Grove's waiting list and waited seven years!

It was over a period of fifteen years that Carl's and my search for a Life Care Community—a Continuing Care Retirement Community—to call home had stretched. When we finally selected Elm Grove we had already looked at, visited, inspected, and quizzed the administrator and staff at more than two dozen Communities. We thought we had chosen wisely. The superstructure—as far as we could see or were permitted to see—had been carefully checked. But it took almost a year to learn that only by living as a resident in a Community can one gauge the infrastructure—the demeanor and posture of the administration, the staff, and the residents—to learn that faith and trust in choosing such a Community can be worthless.

Would that at our interview in June prior to our move into Elm Grove the administrator had said, "Mrs. Lindstrom, Life Care Communities are not for everyone—perhaps you would be happier somewhere else!"

When Carl and I vacated Elm Grove, among the remarks tossed at us by some residents as we left were, "You looked at two dozen Communities before coming here. You should have looked at just one more!"

CHAPTER II

"YOU'RE TOO FUSSY!"

It was the last week in October 1989 when Carl and I received a call in Sun City, Arizona from Elm Grove's admissions director, saying that a two-bedroom/two-bath apartment was going to be available. Would we accept it sight unseen or would we prefer to come East to look at it? I had her word, she said, that it had a prime location—it overlooked the woods. We chose to see it for ourselves because many of the apartments at Elm Grove overlooked carports as well as the woods and were close to buzzing electrical units.

One would think that two people who had researched more than two dozen Life Care Communities, who had asked pertinent and impertinent questions along the way, and who had sold real estate for several years would have had the good sense to question, carefully, everything we saw at Elm Grove when we arrived to inspect the apartment offered. Excuses are not acceptable, but if I had to offer one it would be that we had put great faith in this administration.

The resident, who had occupied the unit since the opening of Elm Grove almost ten years ago, had not as yet vacated the premises. He had been transferred to Laurel House, Elm Grove's personal care facility, but his belongings had not been removed. He sat in their midst with walking aides nearby while a young man packed books under his watchful eye. It was through this clutter that the admissions director gave us an inspection tour of the apartment. The entire place was badly in need of cleaning, the carpeting was soiled and ripply, the walls were dingy.

Did we ask, "Are you going to clean this apartment properly? Are you going to replace the badly chipped sink in the bathroom? Are those worn-out drapes going to be replaced?" No, we didn't, for we took for granted that Elm Grove was anxious to turn over this apartment quickly and that was the reason it was being shown to us in such a state. We assumed that the apartment would be cleaned and ready for occupancy just as soon as the elderly occupant was settled in Laurel House.

My husband and I had spent more than sixteen years in Sun City, Arizona where much emphasis had been placed on things sparkly and new. Concurrent with our inspection tour of our future home our next door neighbors in Sun City were moving to a Life Care Community in Peoria, Arizona and Lynn was eagerly awaiting their move-in. Her chosen community had been built ten years ago, so it was of the same vintage as Elm Grove. However, before the Klines' move-in, the Peoria administration had taken out all the cabinets in kitchen, baths, and utility room to refinish them; had installed all new appliances, i.e., stove, dishwasher, refrigerator, disposal, water heater—for, after all, those appliances were now ten years old with ten-years' worth of use. New carpeting of their choice had been laid as well as new flooring in kitchen and baths, the walls were painted to their specification, and new draperies were hung. Said Lynn with stars in her eyes, "It's like moving into a new house!"

And well it should be. The original prices of accommodations in these ten-year-old Life Care Communities had more than doubled over the years. One could expect that when one pays twice as much for a unit as the price it brought ten years ago it should be refurbished to look like a new unit.

So Carl and I weren't at all concerned about this ten-year-old unit we were inspecting in Elm Grove—our prospective home. Surely it would look like new when we moved in.

The admissions director, Carl and I stopped for quite a while in the kitchen. I told the director I would like a dishwasher and asked for permission to install one. She tried to discourage this by saying that I didn't need one. "You," said she, "won't need to cook." She continued by saying that Carl and I would eat all our meals in the Elm Grove dining room or coffee shop, that I would have more interesting things to do than to cook when I moved in. My answer to that was that I liked to cook and entertain, that cooking was a hobby and moving to Elm Grove didn't mean I was giving up all the things I enjoyed. She conceded that some Elm Grove residents had dishwashers and I took this as acquiescence.

After we had seen the layout of our prospective apartment, my husband and I accompanied the admissions director to her office to discuss carpeting and the color of the walls. We asked if we could install a gray berber carpet rather than the lesser grade, beige-colored one Elm Grove supplied. The director said that if we wanted a different color and kind of carpet we would have to pay for it. This was a satisfactory answer for Elm Grove was going to be our home—we were perfectly willing to pay for it. "Berber carpeting is a very wise choice," said she. "I have that kind in my home and it will last for years." She added that she would arrange for the person with whom Elm Grove contracted for the provision and laying of carpet to bring samples and meet with us in the game room downstairs. We chose a gray berber carpet and contracted for it to be laid. There was no carpet allowance and we asked for none.

Next we asked if we could have the walls painted to match the carpet. Yes, if we paid for the paint. Elm Grove's painter, however, would apply the paint. Again we agreed for this was going to be our lovely home for years to come.

We didn't ask if cabinets in the kitchen would be refinished, if the badly chipped sink in the bathroom which had been mended with daubs of white appliance enamel would be replaced, or if the defective sliding door in the living room would be taken care of because this was part of getting the apartment ready as far as we were concerned. We were told it would take six weeks for Elm Grove to ready our unit for move-in and we returned to Sun City to prepare for the move.

It was on December 11 amid a snow storm that we flew into Philadelphia; the furniture was to arrive the weekend of the 16th, the 18th at the latest. It arrived on the 15th. Our carpet was lovely, the walls just the right color; but the bathroom cabinets still sported their original 10-year-old yellow paint now etched with many streaks and badly faded. I asked the painter, after complementing him on the lovely job on the rest of the apartment, why the bathroom cabinets had not been finished since all the doors, frames, and walls were clean and bright. He replied, "The Maintenance Department said they were not to be painted. They were OK the way they were because the fiber glass tub and shower are not gray. "But," he continued, "if you really want them painted I can come when I'm finished work and I'll paint them for you. It will cost you, however, $5 for each cabinet." It would have cost $10 for a brush for Carl to do it himself so we told the painter to come and we paid him the $10.

I'm sure it was prior to the arrival of our furniture, when I was lining bathroom shelves, that I came into the kitchen to find Carl scouring dirt and corrosion around the sink. When I asked what he was doing he said that he had hoped to get this cleaned before I saw it. I told him to stop immediately—I was going to the Maintenance Department—we had no business doing their job!

Carl had already been to the Maintenance Department to ask if they intended to replace the badly chipped sink which had been repaired so often in such a sloppy manner. I, too, had asked the housekeeper if she couldn't clean out the cinders and dirt from the bottom of the kitchen utility closet where the previous occupant had apparently kept his boots; and I had also called Housekeeping to ask if we weren't supposed to have some drapes at the bare windows. The answer, "Well, Mrs. Lindstrom, with that beautiful carpet and gray walls I didn't think you'd want these old drapes!" I said that I certainly didn't want old drapes but I had to have something at the windows until I got some I did want.

And the ones she hung were old ones that appeared to have been washed many times.

So with fire in my eyes I again went to the Maintenance Department where I encountered the Buildings and Grounds administrative assistant. I told her I had just found Carl attempting to clean the dirt from behind the faucet in the kitchen and I had stopped him. I said that the ten-year old kitchen sink was marred and scratched, that the faucet was corroded, and I wanted a new sink! The maintenance supervisor was passing by at that moment and the administrative assistant said to him, "This is Mrs. Lindstrom, our new resident. She would like to have a new sink in her kitchen." Said the supervisor, "What's wrong with the sink?" I replied, "It's marred and scratched and cruddy and I think that after ten years it should be replaced. I want it replaced even if I have to pay for it!" The maintenance supervisor turned on his heel, and, as he walked away from me, said over his shoulder, "Well, we'll do anything you want so long as you're willing to pay for it!"

I returned to the apartment, furious, to report this to Carl and when one of the maintenance workers, a pleasant, courteous, and efficient young man, came to measure the sink for size I told him that since I had to pay for the new sink I wanted a double, almond one to match the appliances—not a stainless one. All this happened during the middle of December. We were settling for this nonsense since, as I've repeated, this was going to be our home for many years and it would be made to look like a home in spite of the intimidating demeanor of Elm Grove!

Before the end of the week we came out of the dining room one evening to find this note in our mailbox:

"Evidently you have not been properly advised. For the dinner meal, the dining room requires men to wear ties and jackets. For those that prefer not to wear ties, the coffee shop is always available."

Carl was hurt—I could tell by the expression on his face. He shredded the note without letting me read it. I caught the pieces as he dropped them in the wastebasket and I taped them together. Carl declared, "I will never go into that dining room again as long as I live here!" It must be explained that Carl was dressed in suit jacket, neatly pressed trousers, dress shirt, polished shoes, but instead of a conventional necktie he wore a beautiful silver Hopi bola, the neckwear of our country's Southwest from where we had come and where we had lived for twenty years.

The next morning I took Carl's note to the office of the admissions director to tell her that if a bola were good enough for the floor of the United States Senate (Goldwater had read into the *Congressional Record* that a bola is the official neckwear of Arizona. He, himself, even wore one with formal attire), it was good enough for Elm Grove's dining room.

She conferred with Mr. Near, Elm Grove's administrator, and Carl and I were called to his office. Mr. Near said that this was not Elm Grove's way of doing things and besides, there was no dress code for the dining room. He offered an apology on behalf of all of Elm Grove's residents. But, to the day we left Elm Grove, Carl and I could not go to the dining room and share a table with others chosen by the dining room hostess without wondering if the person across from us were the rude character who had written that note.

There was a time, however, shortly after this incident when Carl and I alone, with no welcoming hosts, returned to the dining room. We asked the hostess to be careful where she placed us for we didn't wish to offend anyone. She indicated that she knew the reason for our request and she complied by seating us at a table with an elderly woman who was partially blind and another resident from the sheltered care section who was a very early Alzheimer's victim—both enjoyable, both without predilection, but I'll wager the hostess didn't seat us there for that reason.

The common laundry serving our apartment complex was filthy! Before I washed my clothes the first time after move-in, I used a whole bottle of cleaning fluid and wore out three old tooth brushes cleaning behind and under the lid and rim of the washer I intended to use. Time and again I would go back to my apartment for my mop to clean the floor in front of the dryer and washer I was using just in case I dropped a garment on the floor. Finally, toward the end of December, I was in the laundry with Mrs. Bates, a longtime resident, when a housekeeper came in to flip her mop around. This was the conversation that ensued:

Mrs. L:	How often do you clean behind and under these machines?
Housekeeper:	Oh! we aren't supposed to move the machines!
Mrs. L:	I didn't suppose you were, but how often are they moved out?
Housekeeper:	I don't know.
Mrs. L:	How long have you been here?
Housekeeper:	Two years.
Mrs. L:	And how many times have they been pulled out in two years?
Housekeeper:	None.

Now Mrs. Bates had been taking this in, so she got in the act.

Mrs. Bates:	These girls work very hard!
Mrs. L:	I didn't say they didn't.
Mrs. B:	If you expect them to do any more you'll drive up our maintenance fee!
Housekeeper:	Yes, I don't get paid enough now!
Mrs. L:	(to Mrs. B) Let me tell you something, my dear. If you think your maintenance fee is high now you just let this place get any seedier and the first thing you know it will look like Spruce River, we'll lose our waiting list, and then you just watch our fee go up!

And I barged out of the laundry room to the office of the admissions director. I told her that I had just had an encounter with an old resident and I didn't come to offer an apology, for the laundry room is a disgrace! It isn't fit to work in! I had come to her with a proposition. The maintenance supervisor had told me that Elm Grove would do anything I wanted done so long as I was willing to pay for it. I didn't want Mrs. Bates' maintenance fee to go up—I didn't want anyone's fee to go up just because I like my laundry clean. I offered to pay the maintenance men to pull out those machines and I'd give up my weekly apartment cleaning so that housekeeping could use my time to clean out the dirt. That was my proposition.

The admissions director looked shocked and said, "You shouldn't have to do that!" I agreed, but said I was willing. So she said, "Let me talk to Mr. Near and I'll get back to you."

After she and Mr. Near had toured the laundries of Elm Grove, she telephoned me as she had promised. She said, "Virginia, you had a legitimate complaint and your laundry was the worst. Now it will be taken care of—it won't be tomorrow, it probably won't be this week, it might not be this month. But we'll take care of it." Months went by. Some of the lint which could be reached had been cleaned out, but the machines were not moved, the dirt was still there. One old, broken-down machine was replaced. I had asked the housekeeping supervisor for a broom and dust-pan to be put in the laundry closet so that, for those of us who were so inclined, we could sweep the lint from the floor without going back to our apartment for such equipment each time. These were provided. All in all, that was the sum of "taking care of it".

Back to our apartment. Carl and I were slowly getting our cartons unpacked. The dark kitchen really disturbed me so we went to a home improvement center nearby and purchased a long, four-tubed, fluorescent light fixture. An Elm Grove mainte-nance man removed the small recessed light in the ceiling which had only a single incandescent bulb, returned it to the adminis-tration, and installed the new fixture we had bought.

Now we could see what Elm Grove had given us in our kitchen. The doors on the kitchen cabinets were in need of refin-ishing. Some, especially those beneath the sink, had the finish scoured off. We bought a small bottle of stain to cover the edges of doors which had been scrubbed white. I scraped years of dirty wax from the edges of the cabinet bases at the floor. The oven of the range would not maintain the temperature set. The refrigera-tor froze fresh vegetables when we tried to keep the vegetables fresh and crisp. Shelves were missing in the pantry. The sink we ordered hadn't arrived. Elsewhere in the apartment the dual panes of the sliding doors in the living room entrapped moisture and, combined with the dust, ran down in unsightly streaks. The drapes hung limp and uneven.

But it was the food preparation and menus of the kitchen at Elm Grove that precipitated my first summons to the dietitian's office. As a result of Carl's initial physical examination at Elm Grove it was determined that his cholesterol level had elevated drastically in just three months. The nurse practitioner in Resident Health told Carl that she wanted him to keep a record of what he ate for a week and bring her a list of a week's worth of meals. When he objected saying that he and I had been following, for years, the diet regimen prescribed by our physicians in Sun City, of eating our heavy meal at noon and a light meal in the evening, she said that Elm Grove's menus were varied enough to enable him to find some foods at any time to accommodate his needs. He told her he would give me the task of keeping the record since, for years, I had monitored his diet and kept his cholesterol level in check. He returned to the apartment to tell me about the meeting.

The record was kept and submitted to the nurse practitioner the following week as requested, but I had to challenge the statement that Elm Grove's kitchen prepared a menu varied enough to accommodate our needs. First of all, the main meal—the heavy one—was served at night and this in itself did not agree with our prescribed regimen. So along with Carl's record of food consumed I sent the following letter.

March 23, 1990

Dear Nurse Practitioner,

Carl came back from your office last week to announce that his cholesterol had climbed to 260 during the past three months and said I was to keep a record of everything he ate for one week. (Enclosed you will find the record.)
I was disturbed, perhaps more than you, for I have worked hard monitoring Carl's diet for the past three years—probably the reason why he said that I was to keep the record. For three years I have told him what he could and could not eat. He also told me that you said Elm Grove's menus are varied enough so he should be able to eat a cholesterol-free meal. Have you studied the menus? Have you researched the preparation? I'll give you a rundown of this past week.

Sunday (Main Meal)

Prime Rib of Beef
Broiled Swordfish
Cranberry Orange Chicken*

*Heart-safe—which we ordered. When we removed the skin the grease oozed out and ran onto the plate! No way is chicken "heart safe" when the skin is cooked with the fat entrapped to permeate the chicken.

Monday (Dinner)

Baked Blue Fish*
Zucchini Parmesan
Mushroom quiche

We chose the quiche even tho' it is made with milk and eggs. Why? We have found the kitchen's blue fish unpalatable. It has an odor. Passing people in the hall taking dinner to their apartments you can smell fish even in closed containers. Also, the one time we ordered blue fish in the dining room it was not firm, but rather mushy. A sign fish is not fresh. And fresh fish has no odor—ask Julia Childs.

Tuesday (Dinner)

Roast chicken quarter*
Homestyle beef pot pie (swimming in gravy)
Baked omelette (eggs and milk again)

*Again we chose the chicken. Again we removed the skin and again grease oozed out.

Wednesday (Dinner)

Roast Beef with Pan Gravy
Barbecued spareribs were substituted for
cinnamon apple pork*
Grilled cheese and tomato

The roast beef with no gravy (in which case it is cold) was the least of three evils.

Thursday (Dinner)

London Broil au Jus
Shrimp Broccoli Stir Fry*
Spaghetti and Meatballs

Carl is allergic to shrimp. Elm Grove's spaghetti is too acidic. Beef again? We settled for $1/2$ baked potato and 3 spears of asparagus.

*Heart safe

Please, don't tell me that Elm Grove's diets are varied enough to allow for a cholesterol-free meal (unless, of course, you eat only vegetables and forget the entree.) I've studied too many books on nutrition to accept that. I know that the fat and sugar-laden desserts are a no-no, but it's the one thing Elm Grove's kitchen is really good at and I'm not going to nag Carl about eating them.

Sincerely,
Virginia K. Lindstrom

The dietitian's first comment upon opening my meeting with her was, "Mrs. Lindstrom, are you an activist?" I had not voluntarily activated anything. My letter to the nurse practitioner was merely an answer to her request. But the dietitian's question was polite and not confrontational so I said, "No. But if ever I see anything unfair or unjust I wouldn't hesitate to speak out." She didn't seem to view my letter to the nurse practitioner as criticism, but looking back, I'm sure the administration did.

After an interest in Carl's and my regimen, the dietitian went on to say she thought I might get some of Elm Grove's residents together in little groups and tell them why they should eat their heavy meal at noon and a lighter meal at night just as Carl and I had done. Perhaps, if convinced, they would spread the word. My answer to that suggestion was that what the other residents did was none of my business—I was only concerned about Carl and me. I really thought it was her place, not mine, to reeducate the residents of Elm Grove if such were on her agenda. But I refrained from saying so.

Thus arose, as I look back on this conference with the dietitian, a silent seething that erupted months later in a contemptuous tantrum by the administrator at our September meeting:

"Elm Grove never said it prepared cholesterol-free meals!"
"We will not change Elm Grove's regimen just to suit you!"
"We feed mainstream and you undoubtedly do not fit in
the mainstream!"

I'm sure I had fallen into disfavor when I marched to the office with Carl's nasty pre-Christmas note telling him to stay out of the dining room if he wouldn't wear a conventional necktie. I compounded the disfavor, I'm sure, by fussing about the apartment that hadn't been readied for us. I certainly won no brownie points by criticizing the filthy laundry. And now with my letter of criticism about the food I was really a thorn in the administrator's side else why would he have stored up remarks for September that had their foundation in the letter—my March letter to the nurse practitioner?

Let it be noted that as a result of the meeting with the dietitian there was no offer on her part, or on the part of the nurse practitioner, to assist in satisfying Carl's and my dietary need within the framework of Elm Grove's food service. The nearest we came to assistance was from the medical director, but that, too, came to nothing.

Carl's consultation with the nurse practitioner had been a follow-up of his physical examination by the Elm Grove medical director. Not in the manner of a preconceived complaint in any way whatsoever, but merely in response to a question put to him by the medical director concerning his and my diet at Elm Grove, Carl quoted the prescription of our past physicians for a heavy meal at noon and lighter meal in the evening. Carl then explained that although he and I had tried, we found the Elm Grove's menus could not accommodate us.

From the medical director there was none of the intimidation Carl and I had grown to expect from almost all the staff at Elm Grove. He understood without argument and said he would ask the administration to remove Carl and me from the mandatory food-payment plan, thus allowing us freedom to pursue our diet regimen without paying for food we could not eat. However, Carl never received word that the administration had accepted, or denied, the medical director's request; or if the medical director had presented it at all. Carl did not pursue the point—he decided that we would continue on our own just as we had been doing without bothering anyone in Elm Grove, especially since no one seemed to care. We knew that our plan was fine for now but what about the future if we were incompetent patients in Ashley House, unable to fend for ourselves? Six months later, in September, we had our answer.

On February 20, 1990—just ten weeks into our residency at Elm Grove—Carl and I received a notice in our mailbox informing us that Elm Grove was planning to sponsor a series of brainstorming sessions in cooperation with the Residents Association to solicit recommendations and ideas for projects that may be pursued to strengthen Elm Grove's programs and position by the year 2000. "Project 2000" it was to be called.

The notice consisted of three different inserts. The first of these, addressed to "Resident" and signed by the Planning Committee read, in part, as follows:

Dear Resident:

You are cordially invited to attend a brainstorming meeting on Monday, March 5, in the Game Room – 9:00 to 10:15 A.M. As the second step in our planning process, each resident is being encouraged to think about the outside forces that will prevail upon our Community in the next decade. . . . All thoughts will be recorded for review by the Planning Committee. An agenda is included to help you begin to formulate your thoughts. We look forward to your participation.

Sincerely,
The Planning Committee

The second sheet included responses from various committees of the Residents Association which were of concern to members of the committees themselves. These included quality of life and were expressed, in part, as:

"Many committees noted their deep sense of pride in the quality of life engendered by our unique community. Loving concern for continued human, physical and spiritual well-being was frequently expressed. A caring staff, friendliness, participatory decision-making, and well-kept facilities are some of our Community's treasured assets, which the Community must maintain and perfect."

The part of that paragraph, in light of our experiences, that dealt with well-kept facilities needed addressing, I felt. And the third enclosure convinced me that I was right. For this enclosure read:

Resident Meetings
Agenda

"One way to look at Elm Grove in the year 2000 is to consider three facts. One is the rapid development of life care communities in the United States. In 1980 there were 400; there are now 800 and it is estimated that there will be 1,600, both for-profit and nonprofit, by 2000.

The second fact is that Elm Grove has a waiting list of about 700 applicants, from which we draw about 20 to 25 each year. Right now we have considerable demand; however, some think that the waiting list may be very fragile.

The third fact is evident in the immediate environment around Elm Grove. As residential and commercial development occur there is increasing demand for labor. Increasing demand for labor means higher wages. The effects of this have been seen at Elm Grove more and more during the past five years. In light of the above the planning committee would like to put three questions to the residents:

In the next ten years how should Elm Grove respond to the predictably increasing competition within the life care industry?

What will be the impact on Elm Grove if another life care community is built near us?

The competition for labor is bound to become more severe and Elm Grove is going to face some difficult choices: should services be cut back or should maintenance costs continue to rise?

The Planning Committee believes that change is inevitable in the next decade. The challenge is to foresee and manage events to the best of our ability so that change will be good for Elm Grove as well as helping us in a competitive position."

My husband and I read and reread these enclosures and struggled with them. We had been residents for only ten weeks, but we already were aware, regardless of the rhetoric expressed in the agenda for "Project 2000," that most residents were content with things as they were—things had enough "excellence" as they stood, everything was "good enough".

Additions, and additions planned with the primary motive to entice new residents and thereby stay competitive may be necessary. But how about "excellence" in what Elm Grove already had? "Good enough" is not "excellence". When Carl and I left Elm Grove we were accused by the administrator of having expectations that Elm Grove was unable to produce. But hadn't it touted itself as "The Cadillac" of retirement communities?

The Elm Grove that had impressed us when we selected it to be our home, and during interim visits while we waited for admission, was not the Elm Grove we were observing and experiencing now. There had been a change in administration two years before our move-in, and with it came a change in demeanor and posture of administration—the present Elm Grove, it seemed to us, did not care, or did not have the capacity, to strive for "excellence", except, perhaps, in its desire for national recognition. Instead, it satisfied itself with procrastination and a philosophy of "good enough".

Should we tell the residents who would be gathered at the brainstorming session to which we were invited to bring our ideas just how we felt? How Elm Grove compared with newer, as well as older, Communities which throbbed with ambition to excel? I would go to bed each night rolling this question over in my mind. Then on February 25 in the magazine section of the local paper, there appeared an article which gave me the moral fortitude to express what was bothering me.* The last paragraph of this lengthy discourse, I thought, was most apropos.

The author, after condemning incompetence in every form throughout the article, challenged the reader to be courageous

---

* "Can't We Do Anything Right? How Incompetence Is Destroying America" by Art Carey, *Philadelphia Inquirer*, 25 January 1990.

enough to insist on quality and excellence in everything and to be willing to attempt to make the good better and the better best. For, he concluded with the challenge that we owed this to those who had preceded us, but we owed it more to those who, coming after us, were depending on us. I decided to open my remarks at that Project 2000 meeting by reading that final paragraph in its entirety.

Thus began my public expression of my feelings about Elm Grove—and my belittlement among those who heard. Quoting an old cliche, "I had strode where angels fear to tread," as I told Elm Grove residents and administrators gathered there what a prospective resident, ten years hence, would expect from Elm Grove as he was admitted to the independent quarters based on what we knew from personal experience. I didn't say that was what Carl and I had expected when we entered Elm Grove, but I'm sure the administrative staff gathered there got the message. The moderator asked for the page which I had typed and from which I read my remarks and did not return it. But I was right. I had made many of those at that session unhappy. The conclusion voiced by the gathering was summed up in a resident's final remark, "We're already the best. What's there to do?"

Most of those at that session were pushing eighty years of age or better; most would not be here in the year 2000 whereas I expected to be. I wanted my investment protected and secure. I had something to lose by the "business as usual" and the "good enough" philosophy of Elm Grove. I had to speak out.

Some time after this brainstorming session I stumbled upon a letter which had been stashed in an obscure place on the bottom shelf of the Elm Grove library. It had been written by an early resident about a similar session in a prior year. The resident, who had been inspired just as I had been by a passage of an author, began her letter by defining a "true community" as had been spelled out by that author at an earlier time. Her "true community" was one, she said, that should be big enough to allow for self-criticism; one that would not feel that it was necessary to remake the world in its own image. She asked that Elm Grove reflect this philosophy.

In her letter she wrote of a report which had summarized the conclusions of the residents at a meeting she had attended, and she deplored the lack of complaints in pronouncements delivered by the assemblage. "Only a few people complained!" the report had stated with pride, emphasizing the accolade twice. "We came off with flying colors," was the comment of one of the residents about the report. "Thus," said the writer of the letter, "it was implied that complaints are bad, that right-minded people do not complain or point out what is unsatisfactory." To the letter writer, the report was an example of parochialism and censorship in an attempt to make a good impression. Her input which contained critical comments, as well as that of others which were not the kind that extol, was quashed and not published.

She wrote, "When there are things wrong, we would do better if the wrongs were admitted and efforts made to correct them. We should be mature and strong enough to respect the minority as well as the majority view."

Her dissensions and philosophies had been buried on an obscure bottom shelf of Elm Grove's library—flattering compared to the disposition of my remarks. For when the summary of all the meetings of "Project 2000" was published and placed openly in Elm Grove's library not a single suggestion of mine was included.

Following that brainstorming meeting, Carl decided that he had tolerated Elm Grove's procrastination long enough—we had been residents for three months which, to his way of thinking, was time to make our domicile look like a permanent home. So on March 8 Carl, in frustration, sent the following letter to Mr. Near:

March 8, 1990

Dear Mr. Near:

You have said at various meetings that I have attended, "Bring your grievances to the administration."

A. The window on the oven door in our apartment is defective. Maintenance attempted to replace the door, but the replacement-to-be was not the correct size. The dual panes were removed and the window cleaned (a thorough and efficient job). However, the streaks will continue to appear, although the oven has not been used since move-in day, because Maintenance says the streaks are cleaning fluids that seep in when the cleaning personnel clean the oven door. Virginia, each week, must remind the cleaning girl not to get the fluid near the glass—a reminder that sometimes goes unheeded. Am I to accept a defective door with a broken seal that is in need of constant monitoring because "it passed inspection and is good enough"?

B. The sliding door to the veranda is streaked with muddy rivulets that cannot be cleaned because they are between the dual panes and apparently the result of seeping dust and condensation. A request for a determination as to what can be done was provided Maintenance weeks ago, but there has been no response. Am I to peer through an unsightly window forever because "it passed inspection and is good enough"?

C. On move-in day, Dec. 15, the kitchen sink around the faucet was so cruddy I could not remove the built-up grime. The sink bottom is scratched as a 10-year-old-hand-me-down would be. Maintenance replaced the faucet and cleaned out the crud but refused Virginia's request to replace the sink. I agreed to replace the sink at my expense. The sink size was measured but to date there has been no response. Am I to accept this 10-year-old-hand-me-down sink because "it passed inspection (even with the crud) and is good enough" even though I am willing to have it replaced at my expense?

D. The apartment was painted gray before move-in (a good job). I paid for the paint (no grievance). The walls of each bathroom were painted gray also. The cabinets below each sink had the 10-year-old yellowish color and dull appearance that one would expect to occur over that time. Maintenance refused to paint the cabinets gray even with the paint I purchased because "they had passed inspection and were good enough". I had them painted gray by paying for the job.

E. Over the past 10 years the varnish has been scrubbed off the drawers in the kitchen. It would have been nice if Maintenance had dabbed just a little varnish on those drawers but then of course, these, too, must have "passed inspection" and consequently were considered "good enough". Am I to believe that will be done at my expense if I wish to have it done?

If these grievances are unreasonable, please advise me so that I may understand Elm Grove's policies regarding such situations.

Respectfully,
Carl A. Lindstrom

And so, on March 12, Mr. Near and the admissions director, in answer to Carl's letter, came to the apartment. Carl wanted the sink we had requested in December and for which we would pay; dust between the dual panes of the sliding door removed or the door replaced; a new oven door since the old one was not sealed properly so that I had to tape a permanent note on the door, as the Elm Grove maintenance men had suggested, to remind the housekeeper not to get cleaning fluid near the pane of glass because it would leak through making the view window look as though grease were running down the inside. Carl asked that just a "little bit" of varnish be applied to the kitchen cabinets. He told these administrators about all the problems we had when we moved in—the apartment, other than the laying of the carpeting and the painting of the walls, had not been readied for us. The kitchen and bathroom floors had not been cleaned and waxed. He explained how a maintenance worker slopped a dirty mop over the kitchen floor and onto the beautiful carpeting as he waxed before we could stop him. We had to request that the chipped, unsightly, and badly repaired bathroom sink be replaced. We had to request drapes for the windows. No! This apartment definitely had not been readied for us when we moved our furniture and belongings 2000 miles across the country in the dead of winter. Mr. Near sat silent and poker-faced through the recital, but the admissions director said, "I don't understand why all these things weren't taken care of. This shouldn't have happened. All I can say is for some reason or other this apartment just fell through the cracks." Did it really? The Buildings and Grounds director said that I was too fussy! "That isn't bad, mind you, but you're too fussy!"

After they left, the director of Buildings and Grounds was sent to our apartment. There was nothing wrong with the oven door. According to him, all ovens in Elm Grove were like this. The double almond sink obviously had not been ordered but he said that he would give us a new stainless, single sink, so I let him put it in resolving to myself that I'd give it back when I got the dishwasher and double, almond one. There was no comment about the cabinet doors needing a little varnish. Within days we had the sliding door repaired. With the apartment refurbished, as much as Elm Grove was going to do, and the boxes unpacked I was ready to volunteer my services in Elm Grove's skilled nursing section, Ashley House, at the end of March.

But all was not smooth sailing yet. In the Elm Grove Bulletin on March 30 there was an article saying Lamont Awning Company would, as of the middle of April, begin putting up awnings which had been stored for the winter. If residents had any questions they were not to bother Maintenance; rather, they should call Lamont Awning Company directly. Our apartment had, on the balcony, the framework for an awning. So, following directions, we visited Lamont Awning Company and made arrangements for a new awning to be made, delivered, and put in place. We deposited $165.

Several weeks went by and the admissions director called— she was peddling the previous occupant's awning. I told her that Carl and I had followed directions provided in the Bulletin and had arranged with Lamont Awning Company to have a new awning made for us. "Oh, call them and cancel the order!" she exclaimed. I replied, "We can't do that. Carl and I would lose the $165 deposit!"

We received four calls that morning from the office of the admissions director about the previous occupant's awning. Then I discovered, that although I was led to believe that everything attached permanently to Elm Grove's property would be vested in Elm Grove, the framework on the balcony installed by the previous occupant did not fit the mandate. He couldn't sell his awning without the framework! It did no good to point out that the framework was permanently attached to the balcony. So on April 13, Carl wrote a letter to the admissions director:

April 13, 1990

Dear Admissions Director,

There has never been an agreement, written or verbal, that I was to purchase the former occupant's awning and/or framework. For four months there had been no communication initiated by Maintenance who, you indicated, had all the information.

The Elm Grove Bulletin two weeks ago (as did the copy for April 13) stated, "Any questions or problems regarding awnings should be directed to Lamont Awning Company. . . ." This was signed by the Elm Grove director of Buildings and Grounds. I complied. I contracted for a new awning but not the framework. If the framework were the former occupant's and not for my use because it was not vested in Elm Grove, I should have been told so and the framework removed at the time I moved in. I do not want the former occupant's awning nor his framework. I request that Elm Grove or the former occupant remove the framework at no cost to me before April 16 so that I can install my own.

We called Lamont Awning Company and told them to make the framework to accompany the awning we ordered. The total cost was an additional $700. But, then, Elm Grove was our permanent home.

Before going to Ascutney, Vermont for the month of July, we contacted Tofton Kitchen Company about doing something with our dismal kitchen. This was after Sears said that the cabinets in the kitchen might crumble if cut, and therefore they would not assume responsibility for altering a cabinet in order to install a dishwasher. We asked the manager of Tofton Kitchens to visit our Elm Grove apartment and tell us whether or not our kitchen could be modernized. We told him what we wanted, he submitted a plan to us, and we took the plan to the director of Buildings and Grounds. The director was on vacation so we left the plan for him to approve when he returned. On Monday, July 2, he called us at Ascutney to tell us the plan had been approved, but Mr. Near also wanted to make sure that we understood that the new kitchen, once installed, became the property of Elm Grove. I laughed at the question and replied, "When I leave Elm Grove I certainly won't be in any position to take that kitchen with me!" Little did I realize, at that point, that Elm Grove was not going to be my permanent, final home.

We returned August 1—I to my volunteer work at Ashley House, Carl to his many projects he had looked forward to completing. The kitchen wasn't installed as yet because of a strike in the cabinet firm and company vacations. Early in September the old cabinets in the kitchen were removed carefully and returned, screws and all, to Elm Grove. The range, which the director of Buildings and Grounds said was like all other ranges in the Community—none of which then must hold oven heat properly—was returned clean and shiny. And the refrigerator, which froze fruits and vegetables if one wanted the ice cream solid, and made the ice cream soupy if one didn't want the produce frozen, was cleaned and returned to the administration. The director of Building and Grounds had wanted us to go to his supplier to buy a Gibson refrigerator which he said Elm Grove was going to use as replacements for the old GE's, but note, he did not offer us a new Gibson as a replacement for the 10-year-old GE we returned to him. However, the Gibson would have extended beyond our door frame so we replaced the old GE with a '91 model GE—a deluxe number with which I was very pleased.

And now we're on to the September 19 meeting and my mauling in the office of the administrator of Elm Grove.

CHAPTER III

"IT WAS A SUMMONS!"

The admissions director had said, when Carl and I came to Elm Grove in October to look at the proffered apartment, "Oh! you won't want to cook when you get here. You'll find lots of more interesting things to do!" But I wasn't interested in finding "things" to occupy my time. Long before coming to Elm Grove I had decided what I was going to do when I got there.

My wonderful mother, at age 90, had to be placed in the Baptist Nursing Home in Pittsburgh. Blind, with Alzheimer's disease, and paralyzed by a series of strokes, she had to be fed by someone three times a day. For three years, in all kinds of inclement weather, my sister, Dorothy, had gone to the Home almost daily to feed Mother at noon time. As a resident of Arizona I couldn't help, but I promised myself that after settling in at Elm Grove I would feed some elderly patient who had found herself in Mother's situation. I would repay her debt, and mine, to society. So it was in March 1990 when I asked Janice, an Elm Grove resident, where she was going one Saturday evening and was told that she was on her way to Ashley House to help feed some elderly patients, I asked if I could go along. Janice introduced me to Merrie, the charge nurse, who seemed pleased with another volunteer. She asked what night I could help and I responded, "Every night and if I find I can't be here I'll let you know beforehand so you won't be left without a volunteer." Merrie assigned me to help Tricia saying as she did, "Tricia has a great appetite but she chews so slowly it takes a long time to feed her. If you can't give her all of the solid foods be sure she gets all of the liquids for the liquids are very important. I think you'll enjoy the challenge."

And enjoy it I did. I was sure that, as a child, Tricia's mother must have told her to chew each mouthful two hundred times before swallowing, for it took an hour to an hour and a quarter to get Tricia through an appetizer, soup, salad, an entree and vegetables, rolls, dessert, and milk. Long before we were finished, the Ashley House dining room would empty, especially at Merrie's admonition that "the state says anything that isn't eaten in the first thirty minutes will probable not be eaten—it will be cold and unpalatable". So, the half-empty trays would be whisked away, and the patients wheeled back in their gerichairs to their rooms to be put to bed. And Tricia and I would be left alone in the Ashley dining room.

Elm Grove's ambulatory residents had long been enamored of the dinner hour. Each night they would queue up in front of the doors of the main dining room dressed in their finest to eat in little groups of four or six. Dinner, to them, was a festive occasion. So, I took it upon myself to talk to Tricia as someone must have talked to her years before when she, too, was able to go to the main dining room. For a long time I could elicit nothing from Tricia in response, not even a nod of the head. Eventually, however, she would answer with, "No!" or, "Yah!" if asked a direct question. I began each meal by describing what her tray consisted of—for I had a feeling that Tricia was blind—and I would tell her what food was on each spoonful as I brought it to her mouth. Desserts were her favorite food.

I must have been doing a satisfactory job, for after a week the charge nurse asked if I thought I could feed two such patients at the same time. Said Merrie, "It would really be a great help, for

Nellie, too, is a slow eater and has a big appetite." I was willing to give it a try, and I ended my second week at Ashley House with Tricia on one side and Nellie on the other.

Nellie had been a kindergarten teacher and often as she ate she was back in her classroom teaching her "kids". This, at times, made for interesting dinner conversation for when Nellie would say something to this effect, "What's that kid doing back there?" I would reply as though I were participating in the experience, "I don't see him, Nellie. Where is he?" And Nellie might say, "Now he's hiding under his desk!" Then I would assure her that the little rascal just wanted attention and if we ignored him he'd get back in his seat where he belonged. That would mollify Nellie and she would continue eating quietly. The little culprit had disturbed her dinner only briefly.

Sometimes I was "Mother" to Nellie. Sometimes I became "Elizabeth." I could only surmise that "Elizabeth" had been her daughter, for the questions she addressed to "Elizabeth" usually referred to "Elizabeth's" father. "Has your father come home yet?" or "Where did your father go?"

There were times when a ray of sunshine seemed to break through, when Nellie seemed quite lucid and her remarks made absolute sense. Like the night when Mr. Horton and Mr. Vanse were attempting to harmonize at their dinner table in the Ashley dining room while belting out, "Down by the Old Mill Stream". Nellie listened with a frown furrowing her brow and finally blurted out, "I think we have a couple of drunks in here!" Absolutely! There were times when Nellie followed the conversation and the activities around her very carefully.

One night, when she had been given a dish of apricots— boiled, dried fruit with very tough skins—she chewed and chewed and couldn't break up the fiber. The nurse came around with the nightly medication as Nellie chewed and said, "Aunt Nellie, what are you chewing?" And Nellie, disgusted with the whole process, answered sharply, "Chewing gum! What do you think?"

Spinach was on the menu many, many nights and Nellie apparently disliked this vegetable. She was often brought into the Ashley dining room in a gerichair which does not lend itself properly for the handicapped person who is eating nor for the person who is doing the feeding, for that person must bend far over the tray in a back-breaking position. On one particular night I had my left arm resting on the tray of the gerichair and Nellie had a spoonful of spinach fiber squirreled in the side of her jaw. She had grown tired of chewing and had stored it. And with her thumb and forefinger she was investigating my arm resting on her tray.

"What's this?" she asked as she pinched a bit of flesh.

"That's my skin, Nellie," I replied.

"What's it for?" inquired this old teacher, now pupil.

"Well, it covers the muscles and blood vessels and bones, Nellie."

And with this bit of conversation her fingers had worked their way to the bend of my arm at the elbow. While keeping the middle finger of one hand in the hollow of my arm, she removed the spinach fiber from her mouth with the other hand and brought the wad down to the hollow of my arm with the apparent intent of burying it there. She rotated the spinach fiber 'round and 'round as though to say, "So there! That's the end of that stuff!"

Yes, Nellie was an interesting and, at times, an interested patient. Between Tricia and Nellie I really enjoyed my volunteer work. And again, Merrie must have approved of my efforts for she asked if I could find some more volunteers, affirming that they would certainly lighten her job. I tried. I made an appeal to the Residents Association of Elm Grove by letter but there was no reply.

The summer had melted into fall, and as September rolled 'round it appeared to me that Tricia was having problems. When I began to feed Tricia the charge nurse had told me that it was important to feed her all of the liquids on her tray even if I couldn't feed the solids. The liquids were extremely important. Thus far I had managed to give her both. But night after night the appetizer had been a glass of sour canned grapefruit or tomato juice. I noted that Tricia was attempting to rid herself of the straw which I had found to be the best way to feed her liquids. She had a long, sharp nose and an ordinary drinking glass did not lend itself well for me to help her. The nose got in the way, and in order for her to drink from the glass I would have had to tilt her head back far enough to tip the glass so she could swallow. Hence, the straw. But when, after months of feeding, I was aware of Tricia's efforts to rid herself of the straw by pushing it from one side of her mouth to the other, I thought I should communicate my observations to the nurse. So, I asked Drusilla if Tricia had a gastric problem.

"Oh! I don't think so," said Drusilla. "Why do you ask?"

I said that she had been trying to push the straw away when we had acidic juices, yet with milk or the occasional glass of apricot or pear nectar I had no problem, so I was of the opinion that the acidic drinks were bothering her. Too, Tricia belched often, very often, and when I asked if she were full so soon she would say, "No!", but if she belched when I was feeding her the dessert after she had eaten her whole meal and I would say, "Are you full, Tricia?" she would answer, "Yah!" Then I told Drusilla that I had lived with an ulcer for more than fifty years and I knew how the acidic drinks being fed to Tricia would affect me, so I just wondered if Tricia had a gastric problem.

"No," said the nurse. "She's just old. She eats and goes right to bed. She doesn't get any exercise. Old people act this way!"

So much for my practicing medicine. I hadn't said Tricia had a problem. I had merely offered my observations.

And then Tricia, in spite of her capacity to chew, began to choke on the fibers in the food—foods which very often were of poor quality—hard sugar peas, string beans, tough meat, undercooked potatoes. Again, after one violent coughing spell that brought tears down Tricia's cheeks, I spoke to the charge nurse and said that Tricia was having a hard time with the tough fibers. Said Merrie—the same nurse who had told me six months ago that Tricia took a long time eating her dinner—"Well, she probably isn't chewing her food enough!"

I reminded her that that wasn't so. "Do you remember when I told you that Tricia's mother must have told her, as a little girl, to chew each mouthful two hundred times, and she still does? That's the reason it takes so long to feed her."

"In that case," said Merrie, "I guess it's time for pureed food. I'll put it in the report, but the kitchen doesn't always pay attention to me!"

Several nights later, and no pureed food, Tricia choked violently again and I told Bertha, a sweet little nurse who was on duty that night, that I had reported Tricia's choking earlier in the week and the charge nurse said she'd request pureed food, but nothing, so far, has happened. Said Bertha, "I'll put it in the report again but the kitchen doesn't pay much attention to us."

Then I asked, "May I run interference for Tricia?"

"Certainly!" was the reply.

By running interference I intended to find someone who would assure that my friends were given trays with food they could eat with pleasure, and without coughing, choking or belching, even if the kitchen were indifferent to their needs. So I asked, "To whom should I go?" and the nurse replied, "Well, to the dietitian. But don't go tonight for she's busy!"

I, too, was busy for I had a house guest coming from Arizona. Early in my volunteer work the charge nurse had asked what night I could volunteer my services and I answered, "Every night. And if I can't be here I'll tell you well in advance so you won't be surprised if I don't show up." I had alerted Merrie that I would be away for a week; but I, at this time reminded Bertha, too, and told her I would see the dietitian the next week as soon as my house guest left, to ask if Tricia and Nellie could be given foods which they could chew easily and swallow without choking, and liquids they could drink without belching.

However, after going to bed that night I couldn't sleep thinking about Nellie and Tricia. I didn't want the young aides to shovel food into my friends' mouths in thirty minutes as they did with the other patients, so I decided to see the dietitian the next day to request a meeting with her the following week rather than wait to do so after my guest left. I felt an urgency to let the dietitian know what was bothering me, to have her take care of my old friends, and I hoped it could be done sooner than later.

I was aware that Elm Grove's administrator did not approve of residents taking too much of the staff's time, so I decided to type notes from which I could read to the dietitian and thereby limit myself to five minutes or so while I gave her some idea of what I wanted to discuss at the appointment which I intended to make for the following Thursday. At two o'clock in the morning I got out of bed and typed the notes, making no corrections of grammar, spelling, capitalization, or sentence structure. My brain, at times, raced ahead of my fingers on the keys but I was intent on keeping my visit to five minutes, and I didn't want to go off on tangents.

These are the notes I typed and from which I read to the dietitian:

When we talked last March and when I told you that for the past six years Carl and I have eaten our heavy meal at noon, you asked me if I were an activist who might get these Elm Grove residents in little groups and explain why they would benefit from like behavior. I told you, "No. I could care less what these other residents do. It's none of my business."

But since the first of April I have volunteered my services six and seven nights a week (with the exception of July when we were away) in Ashley House feeding old patients who can't feed themselves. The charge nurse assigned Tricia and Nellie to my care—a job which I have taken seriously. I've watched aides in my line of vision as they feed their patients and theirs is but a menial job. Mine is a commitment—a commitment to two old people to whom, whether they know it or not, I have become a friend. And I think they know it for nightly the nurse gives me Tricia's medication because she fights her (the nurse) but takes it easily from me. So, I'm making Tricia and Nellie and Flossie and others whom I have fed the focus of my activism.

Almost nightly Tricia has on her tray a glass of tomato or grapefruit juice. The charge nurse told me when I first started to feed the patients that I was to try to get all their liquids in them even if I couldn't feed the solids. They needed the liquids. But weeks ago I knew the acidic liquids did not agree with Tricia. She lolls the straw around in her mouth—something she doesn't do with her milk nor with the occasional glass of apricot or pear nectar she gets. She belches frequently—not because she's satiated but because she's obviously full of gas. Tricia is a woman of few words but she does say "Yah!" and "No." If I ask while she is drinking the acidic juices if she's full she'll say, "No." When we're almost finished with dessert and she belches and I ask if she's full she'll say, "Yah." Now you wonder, I'm sure, what makes me an expert on acidic foods. I'll tell you. When I was 19, more than 50 years ago, I awoke one night screaming. It felt as tho' a giant hand was tearing out my insides. I was rushed to the hospital and since doctors weren't so sophisticated a half century ago I was operated on for a ruptured appendix. Only there was nothing wrong with the appendix and after an exploratory it was discovered that I had a ruptured duodenal ulcer which had ruptured the bowel. The doctor simply sewed me up, putting in drainage tubes which were in place for three weeks, told my parents he could do no more for me—they'd better pray. Well apparently I was spared for some reason.

For two years I lived on strained baby food, scraped meat and apples, lots of milk and cheese and pudding. And for over fifty years I've treated that ulcer with great respect and it has respected my treatment.

About 15 years ago I developed a hiatial hernia and I found some of the ulcer foods didn't agree with me. I would be wakened with a mouth full of acidic fluid and if I had had a heavy dinner it could come up, not just through the mouth but through the nostrils as well. It was then that I learned that I could eat almost any food at noon when I bustled about all day and I could digest it but I could not eat the same way at night. And although I could drink a glass of tomato or grapefruit juice at breakfast or at noon it was absolutely taboo at night. Those are my qualifications. Fifty years of experience have made me an absolute expert on acidic food. I bow to no one.

Now back to my patients. Here is their tray loaded with food such as these ignorant (and I use this word only because I feel they don't know what they are doing to themselves) diners in the Elm Grove dining room are gorging on, plus acidic liquids which the nurse wants fed.

About a month ago I asked Drusilla if Tricia had a gastric problem after an unusual amount of belching. Drusilla said, "Oh, I don't think so. She doesn't get any exercise and old people are very apt to do this." She doesn't get any exercise and in addition she is taken from the dining room with a stomach full of heavy foods—fried sweetbreads, fried sliced potatoes, cranberry stuffed pork roll and she's put right into bed. If, by the grace of God, I sat in Tricia's chair I'd wake screaming every night! I'd really complicate the over-worked nurses' job!

Two weeks ago Tricia began to choke—often, too often. She had choked before but not so often. Sunday night I asked the charge nurse if Tricia could have some different foods. I said the fibers in green beans, sugar peas, nuts, bits of coconut made her choke. The nurse said, "It's probably time for pureed food. I've requested this time and again but the kitchen doesn't pay attention. But I'll put it down again."

Monday when I went to Ashley they were short of help. The charge nurse had assembled all the patients in that dark TV room opposite the desk. Tricia sat at a table for three and the nurse assigned me Nellie and Flossie to feed. When dinner was over I searched out Tricia's aide and asked if Tricia had had a pureed supper. She said, "Yes", and I was pleased.

But I don't know what happened to the nurse's request because there were no pureed foods on Tuesday night and last night. Tricia choked on bean fibers and nuts in chocolate cake and for a week I've sent back her tomato and grapefruit juices.

To digress a moment, when I fed Flossie on Monday the only liquid she had on her tray was a small glass of juice. I asked the nurse if they had forgotten her milk and Merrie said, "No. She's milk free." I said that Flossie had grabbed the empty glass and ran her tongue around the rim and into the glass as far as she could. And the nurse said, "Yes, I've asked for more liquid but *no one in the kitchen pays attention.*"

When the nurse asked Nellie one night what she had in her mouth Nellie said, "Chewing gum!" I told Drusilla it was apricot skins and Nellie chews and chews and finally I'll say, "Spit it out in the napkin I'm holding, Nellie. You can't manage that!" Drusilla said, "And she gets apricots often!" Indeed she does. Too often. Why can't the apricots be pureed as Mother pureed mine years ago? It's easy now—you use a machine.

I want to know, Belle, why these old Ashley patients can't have a light supper. I don't know what their noontime fare is for I don't have time or energy enough to feed them twice a day.

It takes an hour and fifteen minutes to feed Nellie and Tricia regardless of state recommendations. But if they are being fed a la Elm Grove with a light meal at noon and a five-course meal at night it has to be changed. Going to bed, the patient doesn't need a stomach loaded with enough food to go out and dig a ditch. She doesn't need a piece of pound cake six inches long and three quarters of an inch thick nor a five-inch piece of chocolate cake with nuts. If that was what she wanted when she had all her faculties that's a bygone era: someone responsible has to make her decisions now. She needs something like vanilla pudding—and not laced with mandarin oranges—after a big glass of grapefruit juice and sprinkled liberally with coconut on which she'll choke. And she doesn't need a stomach full of citric acid! Nellie gets, and I feed her, two glasses of acidic food every night. You, as a nutritionist, know I'm right. And if you tell me that you have made recommendations and the kitchen won't follow through you can bet I'm really going to become very vocal as an activist. I shall go to Mr. Near and ask why the kitchen is a law unto itself. And if he doesn't get some action I'm prepared to go to the state and to the federal government. After all, Carl was a PHS officer, Director Grade, an APHA fellow, and we still have some clout in that area. Much is being written these days about the abuse of the elderly. I submit that Elm Grove, even with its caring staff at Ashley House, is guilty of abusing the elderly at meal time. And I'm out to do something about it!

As I read these notes now I can see that they reflected six months of disgust and frustration over the Ashley House dinner hour and Elm Grove's attitude in general. I was angry over the fact that trays sent to the Ashley dining room contained food which elderly patients had difficulty chewing, swallowing, and digesting. I was tired of the cheap, sour grapefruit juice (Oh, I knew what it was like!—I had tasted it once in the Elm Grove coffee shop) which appeared on Nellie's and Tricia's trays time and time again. I resented the old, tough, undercooked, and hard sugar peas, string beans, and cold baked potatoes. And I really resented hearing over and over the admonition that food should be fed to the Ashley patients in thirty minutes.

I realize, as I read them again, there was a great deal of empathy in these notes. I knew that Elm Grove's residents really enjoyed their dinner hour in the main dining room where they sat in groups of four and six chatting to each other as they ate their dinner and stretching out that experience for more than an hour without being admonished to leave early. I didn't know Nellie and Tricia ten years ago but I was sure they, like the present residents, had looked forward each night to the special camaraderie they enjoyed at dinner. Never, I'm sure, in their darkest hour, could they have envisioned what I observed had befallen them now in the Ashley House dining room. This was not the treatment I had expected if ever I were an incompetent or incapacitated patient in Ashley House.

I know why the young aides stirred the pureed foods together—it was so they could spoon the resulting mixture into open mouths in the thirty minute-time limitation they were admonished to spend. Elm Grove touted its "caring, loving" image—but, to me, there was nothing "caring" or "loving" about stirring together pureed beets and spinach and spooning the black goo into an open mouth in a head that was pushed back against the gerichair!

I was tired of this bit that "The kitchen doesn't pay attention!" Why not? Who at Elm Grove was responsible for making the kitchen shape up and pay attention? I intended to rectify this glitch on my own since no one seemed to care one way or the other about feeding patients in a respectful and empathic way—those dear old patients who couldn't speak for themselves. My husband and I had been told in March that our apartment had apparently fallen through the cracks. Was there anyone along the way who was responsible for the preparation, inspection, and serving of the dinner meal to the elderly in Ashley House? Or had it, too, fallen through the cracks? I intended to find out and to do something about it.

So with my notes in hand I stopped at the dietitian's door the next afternoon and asked if I might have five minutes of her time. I said that something was bothering me and I wanted to make an appointment for the following Thursday to discuss it. But in order to have her aware of what I wanted to discuss I had jotted down some notes that would take no more than five minutes to read.

She invited me into her office and I read my notes, finishing sentences that had been unfinished and correcting grammatical errors when I encountered them. When I concluded, she requested the sheet from which I had read. I told her I'd type it over—it hadn't been proofread for I had typed these notes at two in the morning. There were errors, misspelled words, unfinished sentences. It was the thought and not the grammatical construction or spelling I was concerned about last night as I typed.

"Don't worry," said Belle. "I'll be able to decipher it. I just want to be able to discuss your points with you next Thursday." And with that I handed her my notes, she made a copy, and gave me the appointment I had asked for. My Arizona guest was getting ready to leave the following Tuesday when I answered the phone and was told sharply that Mr. Near, Elm Grove's administrator, wanted to see me in his office the next day at 3:30 P.M. There was no asking if I could make the appointment. It was a summons.

I presume I looked a little perplexed when I turned from the phone for Betty said, "What have you done, Virginia? It sounds as though you've been summoned to the principal's office!"

CHAPTER IV

"You're nothing but a volunteer!"

Mr. Near had demanded my presence in his office for a 3:30 P.M. appointment on the 19th of September—just nine months from the date of Carl's and my arrival at Elm Grove. When his secretary called I asked why Mr. Near wanted to see me. She said she didn't know. A few minutes later the administrator, himself, called and said he wanted to discuss the "letter" I had given to the dietitian.

I had not given the dietitian a "letter," there was no "letter," neither had I offered her my notes. Instead, she had snookered them from me on the pretense of needing them to review in preparation for the appointment she had set up for me the following Thursday. But her intent, obviously, had been to hie the copy off to her boss.

"Notes" or "letter"—it made no difference to me. The important thing was that Mr. Near wanted to confer with me. This was great, I thought. He undoubtedly had not been aware of what was going on down in the basement, the location of Ashley House. He hadn't known a "Let Mikey do it" attitude there was depriving patients of the care they should receive at dinner—an attitude which I considered to be sheer indifference and which had led to abuse at meal time. There would be no need now to go through Elm Grove's channels for I had landed at the top quite unwittingly and I was looking forward to this meeting. The dietitian was forgiven for her deceit.

Wednesday morning, before the 3:30 P.M. appointment, I had something important to do. Within the first month of Carl's and my arrival at Elm Grove I had tendered my Living Will as requested by the Social Services director. My feeding of Tricia and Nellie over the past six months had alerted me to the necessity of adding to that document. If ever I sat in Tricia's chair in Ashley House, I could not be fed the foods she was given each night. I knew what foods I could and could not tolerate so I felt an addendum to my Living Will was a necessity. I'd type it, have it notarized, take it with me to my meeting with Mr. Near and ask that one copy be attached to my Living Will and one copy placed in my medical file. Thereupon I typed the following statement in triplicate:

A Memo to Accompany My Living Will

If ever I am an incompetent patient in Ashley House, unable to speak or make decisions for myself and at that time I must be fed by someone, I want my <u>heavy</u> meal at noon, a <u>light</u> meal each night, and at <u>no</u> time any acidic foods which include pineapple/juice, grapefruit/juice, orange/juice. I want no one to feed me any gravies or sauces, and <u>no</u> tomato products in any shape or form. This is for my well-being and to lighten the burden of overworked nurses.

/s/ Virginia K. Lindstrom
Sept. 19,1990

These dietary restrictions and regimen which had been my bible day after day for many years were also those prescribed by a specialist to whom Elm Grove's physician had referred me for medical services just four weeks before this meeting.

Taking three copies of my dietary directive I hurried off to the office of Elm Grove's director of Social Services where I knew the secretary was a notary public. I asked that all three copies be notarized. "Are you sure," asked the secretary, "that you want all three copies notarized? That will be two dollars a copy!" I assured her I had brought my checkbook with me.

Standing behind her desk with my copies in her hand she read the one on top and a smirk spread over her face. I was angry, for I felt she had no right to read any of the copies given her to be notarized even though there was nothing in them that was secret. I had asked her to notarize them, not pass judgment. I said, "Obviously you find this amusing." She retorted, "Well, you sound so adamant about it." I was adamant. If ever I became an incompetent patient in Ashley House I didn't want fed as I was asked to feed Tricia and Nellie and I told her so.

After I had signed the directives and she had placed her seal on them, she grabbed the top notarized document saying, "I'll just put this in our file." I objected, "Please return my addendum! I intend to file it in its proper place!" But before she released it she whirled around and made a copy for her files. I couldn't stop her without creating a scene.

For her files indeed! On my way to keep my 3:30 P.M. appointment with Mr. Near I had a feeling that the notary public, like the dietitian, had gone running with my addendum to "Central Headquarters"—to Mr. Near.

I arrived at Near's office at exactly 3:30 P.M. I didn't intend to be a minute early nor a minute late. When I entered, there, next to Mr. Near, stood Marcie Sharpe, Elm Grove's associate administrator and director of Health Services. No mention had been made of her participation in this conference during the phone calls, and if I had known that this was an ambush I would have had my husband accompany me. "Ambush" is the correct word, for I had barely sat down at the round, glass-topped conference table when Marcie began abruptly, "You had no right to bring out your big guns!" Pent up anger that obviously had been churning for months had finally erupted. I had never talked to Marcie Sharpe, nor with her; nor had I seen her except at Resident Association meetings to which all Elm Grove residents were invited. This was my first eye-to-eye encounter.

I could only assume that "big guns" referred to that part of my notes which I had read to the dietitian where I had said that I was prepared to go to the state and federal governments if Elm Grove would not look into my grievances and correct them. There had been indifference to my observations about the feeding of Tricia and Nellie for weeks. If soliciting governmental help was the only way, after exploring all other channels for me to do something about it, I was willing and ready to pursue that route.

Within minutes of my sitting down at the conference table I realized that any hopes I may have nurtured about getting help for Tricia and Nellie from this office were about to be shattered. These two administrators had no intention of considering the grievances expressed in my notes, there would be no offer to look into them, and if they had merit, there would be no promise to correct them. Rather, from the start, I knew that this conference was to be about me. I was about to be mauled.

Again came, "You brought out your big guns!" more viciously than before. Then Mr. Near closed in, "You have no right to accuse Elm Grove of abuse! We have a good reputation which stretches across the United States. We will not allow you to accuse us of abusing patients. Elm Grove will sue you for this!" This was intimidation. He didn't offer to investigate as to whether or not my grievances were worthy; his intent was to silence me. And if he had stopped right there he may have succeeded, for he took my breath away. I didn't answer—I was shocked. I just looked at him, raised my eyebrows, and shrugged my shoulders to gesture, "Be my guest!", for I didn't know what to say. I was not aware that I had been so scorned by these Elm Grove administrators as their tone and words indicated.

My stunned silence was interrupted with a second threat, "The state could bring charges, too, if you don't feed the patients everything on their trays!" This second threat, I assumed, stemmed from my notation that I had sent back Tricia's tomato and grapefruit juices which she didn't want. The elderly, the incapacitated, and the incompetent are fed in Ashley House dining room. Some patients are ornery, some eat very slowly, some can't chew and swallow the foods provided, some refuse to eat at all. And, yes, a great number cannot finish their dinners in the mandatory thirty minutes allowed. Nightly many trays were removed from the Ashley dining room with the food only half eaten—food that every volunteer or aide must feed to the patients or risk being charged by the state? Indeed! Anger replaced the shock I had felt, but I refrained from comment for I didn't want to infuriate my antagonists any further.

Then again, not from Sharpe this time, but rather from Near himself, I heard, "You brought out your big guns! This is no way to effect change!" I tried to make clear that I intended to go through channels with my grievances. I explained that I planned to go to the dietitian, who, I was told was the correct person to see first; and if she would not, or could not, do anything, then I would proceed to Mr. Near; and if he would do nothing, I would have no choice but to explore the governmental route. I pointed out that Mr. Near had short-circuited me by interfering in a procedure which would have led to an amicable resolution of my grievances by the dietitian and me—no one else would have had to be involved. "But you brought out your big guns!"

I was scolded next for bringing to the charge nurse's attention Tricia's long and slow chewing of fibrous food, and her choking when she attempted to swallow. Marcie snapped, "If Tricia were chewing so much, she wasn't choking because of the fiber!" I wanted to say, but quickly stifled the impulse, "If you concede that Tricia was choking, but not because of the fiber in her food, why haven't you had the resident physician check her?"

Then out of the blue came a rebuke for my asking the nurse if Tricia had a gastric problem. "Since Tricia has difficulty communicating how do you know she resented the citric juices because they disagree with her or because they made her belch so much? You have no right to make such a judgment for Tricia! Her problems are not your problems! You're not a doctor! And there's absolutely no reason why we should consult you—you are not a part of our staff! You're nothing but a volunteer—you are not to make decisions or judgments!" All of this tirade because I had asked Drusilla if Tricia had a gastric problem and had offered my observations on Tricia's reaction to certain foods and citric juices being fed to her. I was being accused of practicing medicine.

My inquisitors, step by step through my notes, admonished, harassed, ridiculed, and belittled me. When Sharpe arrived at my questioning the lack of liquids on Flossie's tray, she chastised me for not bringing Flossie a glass of water. "If you thought she needed more liquid you could have gotten her a glass of water. That would have been the simple thing to do!" she snapped contemptuously. Just moments ago I had been told that I was only a volunteer and could not make decisions. I reminded Sharpe of that. She interpreted the remark as sarcasm and she was right. But it was she who had shot that dart, not I.

I was belittled and intimidated for my recommendations that were expressed in my notes regarding a diet regimen of a heavy meal at noon and a light meal at night for the patients in Ashley House. Near and Sharpe saw this as a demand and roiled in resentment. "The state requires that the patients have 2000 calories a day and that is divided among the three meals," Near piously pontificated, "How could Elm Grove accomplish this state mandate if it changed its diet regimen to the one you are prescribing?"

Diet regimen was then extended to include Elm Grove as a whole. Near declared, "The residents enjoy their dinner just as they have done all their lives! Elm Grove's present regimen will not be changed just for you!" But had I not told Belle last March, at our first encounter, that the residents' eating habits were none of my business? I had never tried to influence those who ate in Elm Grove's main dining room or coffee shop. I had even refused to participate in Belle's sly plan to convince the residents to change their habitual regimen. But I had expressed to Belle that Elm Grove did not accommodate Carl's and my regimen, and Near and Sharpe obviously knew that I had. Yet, I had made no demands. All this occurred six months ago! Had Near's and Sharpe's resentment of me on this issue been festering since last March?

Then followed abruptly and with derision, "Elm Grove never said it served cholesterol-free meals!" With this remark, Near could only be referring to the letter I had sent to the nurse practioner at her request when there was concern about Carl's cholesterol last February. But this, too, was six months ago.

There was no doubt that this confrontation, happening now in September, had been months in the making. With torturous intent it must have been planned, perhaps even rehearsed, waiting for just the right moment to be put into action. My notes to Belle had provided Near and Sharpe the ammunition they had been waiting for. They were treating me like an impertinent kid, but it was they who were having the tantrum.

And then, sandwiched in among all this rage, when I remarked that I alone had fed Tricia and Nellie in the evening, that for six months no one had made the slightest attempt to elicit from me my observations of how they were responding to their dinners, and that no one took notes concerning their behavior, there came this put-down. "The aides take notes constantly! You are not staff! There is no reason to consult you!" The aides Near was referring to were the young, low-paid, high-school and college-age girls who fed the patients in Ashley House and who were constantly being replaced. Then there followed a stunning admission, "Even the cleaning girls take notes and report on what goes on in the apartments!" The apartments Near mentioned are the private accommodations of Elm Grove's residents. Weekly the cleaning girls enter each apartment, clean and dust for about an hour, and change bed linens and towels. So, along with the trash they carry out they also carry tales to be entered in each resident's profile! With all this note taking I could visualize the young woman who often hovered among the diners in the main dining room with pen and black notebook in hand. At times she stood beside my chair, making notations in her book, at other times she quizzed me as to where I had been or made a comment to the effect that "I haven't seen you for a while". I had asked a resident what this girl was doing and I was told that she was keeping statistics on the number of people who ate in the dining room and coffee shop. My retort had been, "Surely the menus we fill out and sign at dinner in the dining room and the check-off in the coffee shop would take care of that—she must have something more productive to do!" Now I knew what this observer with her little black book was up to. Daily my behavior was the statistic, not my body count. In his anger and frustration, Mr. Near was spilling his little secrets.

I tried to present my dietary directive which I had prepared and had notarized that morning—my directive which I hoped, would protect me from being tortured with food and drink that I could not tolerate if ever I became an incapacitated patient in Ashley House.

With only a cursory look, Sharpe contemptuously slid the paper across the glassy surface of the conference table to Near, who, it appeared to me, took time only to glance at the notary seal before skidding it back toward Sharpe. With such an indifferent examination it was obvious to me that they knew the contents of my directive beforehand, and that the secretary in the Social Services Office who provided the notarization, and who made a copy of my directive over my objection, had delivered the copy to Near and Sharpe prior to my arrival for this meeting. The document was immediately subjected to sarcasm and criticism, and deemed not worthy of consideration. Marcie sneered, "This won't do us any good! You tell us what you don't want but you haven't told us what you want!" I explained that it wasn't a matter of want but rather a matter of need, but to no avail. And then she snapped, "Just what do you mean by a 'light' meal?" Struggling to control my anger and feeling the cold perspiration trickle down my back, I replied as calmly as I could, "Well, Marcie, if you don't know, I'm sure the dietitian will." There was no further discussion of my directive.

Near had been sitting quietly through Sharpe's tirade but now, he returned to the fray. "Mrs. Lindstrom, there is something you obviously don't seem to understand. Elm Grove prepares about 350,000 meals a year." Then with hands gesturing in a track-like motion he said condescendingly, "We feed for the mainstream and you obviously don't fit in the mainstream!"

The turn that this conference had taken frightened me! These two individuals had revealed that Carl's and my future health care was in serious danger. Within the hour I had been told with cer-

tainty, by Near and Sharpe to whom Carl and I had given unconditional acceptance to manage our health care destiny in Elm
Grove, that we would not be allowed anyone but staff to advocate on our behalf if ever we became incapacitated or incompetent patients in Ashley House. Carl and I, having no family surrogates, would be at the mercy of Near and Sharpe since it was
now obvious that they looked upon us with indignation and scorn
and had been doing so for some time. Additionally, within the
last few minutes, I was told by these very same custodians that
my dietary directive was not worthy of consideration, and that I
would be fed 'mainstream' as was Elm Grove's custom—a menu
heavy and citrus, tomato, and gravy-laden—and without an advocate permitted, there would be nothing I could do about it as
a helpless patient in Ashley House.

I had watched our future crumble before me. All the reasons
for coming to Elm Grove had been shattered while I sat before
the high court of this institution. But surely Elm Grove's physician
could be reasoned with, so with one desperate attempt to sal-
vage our future I asked, "May I discuss this with Dr. Leo?"

"Absolutely not!" Near shot back, "He's a busy man! His
time is money!" I should have walked out at that very moment
but Sharpe wasn't finished with me.

In machine gun-like succession Sharpe demanded, "Why did
you come to Elm Grove? You could have had a nicer apartment
somewhere else! You don't have anything to do with the residents! You don't engage in any activities with them! You don't
belong to any committees! What have you done for Elm Grove
since you've been here?" I tried to answer the staccato out-
bursts but I was given little time to do so. Sharpe's fury was bub-
bling over like the flow of lava from an active volcano.

My answer to her insulting accusation, "You don't have anything to do with the residents!" was met with belittlement when I
told her that Carl and I attended church services in Elm Hall regu-
larly with the residents; that I had invited our Elm Grove neighbors
for lunch, dinner, and picnic suppers often; that they stopped for
coffee and chats on many an afternoon; that we had never refused to join them in the dining room or coffee shop when we

were invited to share a table; that we had accompanied them on outings to New York, Philadelphia, and the theater. I also told her I wasn't interested in the residents' cocktail parties that preceded dinner—their 'happy hour,' if that was what was bothering her—but Carl and I never refused an invitation when the hostess, learning that we did not partake of alcohol, invited us anyhow.

I could have told her much more if she had given me the opportunity; if she hadn't been so intent on chastising me. To my rejoinder that she could walk down the hall with me and note that I could address residents by name, so how did she think I could associate names and faces if I had nothing to do with the residents, she snapped, "Anyone can do that if he works at it!"

I'm afraid I did bristle at her insolent question, "What have you done for Elm Grove since you've come here?" While she was between breaths I told her, "For the last six months, I have spent an hour to an hour and a half, six and seven evenings every week at Ashley House helping to feed elderly patients who are unable to feed themselves—Tricia and Nellie and others. How much more would you have me do?" I shouldn't have answered that ridiculous question so angrily for hadn't my volunteer work in Ashley House landed me in their office? She knew perfectly well what I had been doing at Elm Grove since last March. By asking that asinine question I knew just how rattled she had become. So consumed with resentment and frustration over being unable to handle one little old lady, unable to break my spirit, and make me yield to their will, she was lashing out wildly, not knowing where her punches landed. I had now taken as much as I intended, so, with a, "Whether you know it or not, Miss Sharpe, there is life outside Elm Grove!", I made a move to leave. She reached across the table top as though to take my dietary directive and I snatched it from her saying, "You don't need this! You said it was useless. I'll just take it and put it where it will do some good!"

I was absolutely certain that this torturous meeting had been premeditated—it had been months in the making. It had started off on a vitriolic note and the hostility had only increased. Although I felt devastated, I had tried desperately not to give evidence of it. I was not going to give them the satisfaction of knowing that they had distressed me. And I must have succeeded otherwise Sharpe would not have ranted like a petulant child, and Near wouldn't have shaken his finger at me saying, "I don't intend to have this conference again!" The iron fist had unclenched, the metallic forefinger was pointed right at me! I smiled and said, "That's fine with me. But I want you to know that the way I felt at two in the morning when I typed those notes was the way I felt when I read those notes to the dietitian, and it is exactly the way I feel right now!" Even though Near had warned me that I was to do what I was told, that I must feed everything on the trays whether or not the patients could eat it, that I had to keep my mouth shut if I wanted to help Nellie and Tricia, I had a feeling that the victory was not theirs. I hadn't gone stumbling from their office in tears. In fact, I went marching out of the office with head high and nary a good-bye.

The outer office was empty and strangely silent, and I wondered where everyone had gone. I looked at my watch—it was exactly 4:45 P.M. and I realized that the encounter had been one hour and fifteen minutes long. The back of my blouse was soaked and sticking to my body. The band of my skirt was wet. I felt numb and weary as I walked down the hall. It was the dinner hour and I know I must have passed and spoken to a number of residents on their way to the coffee shop, but I can't remember that part of the walk. All I could think of was, "What if I had a stroke or heart attack while in that office. Carl would never have known why, but the residents of Elm Grove would have tut-tutted and said, "Wasn't it lucky that it happened where Marcie Sharpe could help her!" I silently thanked God for the stamina and courage to take on these two in one encounter.

In a little more than an hour, Near and Sharpe had wantonly disregarded rights granted to me in state and federal statutes, in policies of the Elm Grove Board of Directors, in promises to the Continuing Care Accreditation Commission when Elm Grove was accredited, in the contractual agreement, and as a citizen of the United States. They denied my right to communicate grievances, observations, and recommendations to them, or any member of the staff, without reprisal, intimidation, and belittlement;

and my right to file complaints with governmental agencies, if that were my desire, without being threatened. Within that hour, they denied my right to advocate voluntarily on behalf of those helpless, incapacitated, incompetent patients who could not speak for themselves in Ashley House; and conversely, denied my right to have anyone, except staff, advocate for me if ever I became an inpatient. And in turn, Near and Sharpe had denied the helpless patients in Ashley House the right to have anyone, except staff, advocate for them.

Near and Sharpe denied my right to be provided assistance in accommodating my dietary needs and concerns. They made no investigation of my complaints concerning food I was given to feed Tricia and Nellie—they only trounced me for making them.

Most importantly, Near and Sharpe denied my right to be treated respectfully, denied my right to independence and self-determination, and denied my right as a citizen of the United States.

Later Carl and I were called confrontational and disruptive to the smooth operation of Elm Grove and were not wanted. But this was after we had made arrangements to leave the Community, and if by saying that, Near and Sharpe thought they were having the last word they were wrong.

CHAPTER V

"It was inevitable"

Approaching the end of my thrashing by Near and Sharpe, after they had admonished me for practicing medicine, for making decisions, for expressing opinions, complaints, and recommendations, I asked if I were being dismissed as a volunteer—that perhaps I should not return to Ashley House. "No! I'm not telling you that you can't go down," said Near, "Your efforts are appreciated, but not your input. We will not tolerate your opinions or criticisms! You are not staff!"

I was torn that night between my continuing with my volunteer work at Ashley House, or quitting. Continuing—returning to Ashley House—won out. I had grown very fond of Tricia and Nellie and they needed help. I'd see that it was forthcoming and in the process I'd help the Flossies, the Dotties, and the Jeffreys, too. If Marcie Sharpe thought for one minute that she was going to break my spirit she had another thought coming. What right did she have to dictate what I could, or could not do, in my own apartment? What right did she have to dictate the activities of my daily life? What right did these two administrators have to deprive me of my individuality, dignity, and privacy, to admonish, humiliate, intimidate, coerce, and harass me to make me bow to their will? By what authority can they take away my rights as an American citizen? I would go back!

As I recalled that night in the quiet of my bedroom Sharpe's questioning Carl's and my fitting into life at Elm Grove, I was infuriated. Why should I have to explain that:

(1)   We had been at Elm Grove less than a week when we had dinner with the Baxters. Mrs. Baxter asked, "Wouldn't you like to run our gift shop?" I had been at Elm Grove only a few days, not long enough to know that the Community was having difficulty finding a volunteer gift shop manager—that none of the residents wanted the job.

I said to her, "Please, let me unpack my boxes before trying to put me to work!" The same person the next week, "Wouldn't you like to head a committee to get a swimming pool at Elm Grove?" I didn't know, at that time, that the swimming pool issue was a devisive one, but I gave her the same answer. These two invitations had been issued in less than one week from the time of my arrival. I was being asked to do those things which no resident wanted to tackle.

(2)   Within the next two weeks I was asked by Mr. Cay if I wouldn't lead their current affairs discussion. Their former leader had quit and they were looking for a replacement. I looked at the man as though he couldn't be serious. With our move from Arizona I hadn't had time to read a newspaper for a month let alone lead a discussion.

(3)   Our first Saturday at Elm Grove, in answer to a knock on the door, Carl was asked if he would take a load of stuff for recycling into Philadelphia. We didn't even know our way around the small adjoining village let alone Philadelphia. We had lived in the desert for twenty years with no driving on icy streets. This was just before Christmas with holiday traffic.

(4)   Same time frame—"We need you and your automobile to deliver meals-on-wheels." On snowy, icy streets, with an automobile and a driver that are not equipped for eastern winters.

(5) I was asked to join the sewing group. I had sewn for the Salvation Army for a number of years in Sun City, but an eye problem doesn't lend itself to such activities any more. When I explained this I heard, "Oh, just come and talk."

(6) Didn't I want to join the exercise class? It meets at 10:00 for thirty minutes. I get up at 7:00 or earlier, I have exercised for forty-five minutes to an hour or more before breakfast in the privacy of my own home. My day began three hours earlier than their exercise class at 10:00.

(7) I certainly wasn't interested in digging in the earth in the garden, for degenerative arthritis in back and hips makes kneeling and bending for long periods difficult.

(8) I refused to sell newspapers. A newspaper box should take care of that chore I thought. There had to be other ways to "meet people".

(9) I have always been an avid reader but, again, my eyes don't lend themselves to reading to myself let alone reading to someone else.

(10) I chose not to assist in Elm Grove's intergenerational program in a private school. Instead, I chose as my own intergenerational program to work with those 85 and 90 year olds in Ashley House who could no longer help themselves. I saw in helpless Tricia my mother who at age 90 had been blind, paralyzed, and a stroke victim. This was my idea of useful volunteerism. I had no need for "things to do".

In the darkness of my bedroom I decided I would keep my appointment with the dietitian the next day and I would go back to Ashley House. I would speak out for Tricia and Nellie and anyone else who might need my help. I would not allow this administrator nor his associate to break my spirit. I would not be intimidated by either—even though they had threatened to sue me.

So promptly at 2:30 P.M. the next day, September 20, I appeared at the dietitian's door to find her waiting. Belle and I had a very pleasant exchange as we should have had with no interference from the administration.

I told Belle, as we began the meeting, that I thought it was unethical of her to go running to Mr. Near before we talked. After all, I was going through channels as I should have done, and she had surreptitiously taken my notes on the pretext that she wanted to answer all of my concerns when we talked again. Seemingly she wanted them for another reason.

Belle offered an apology and then explained, "I was very upset that afternoon for shortly after lunch I got a phone call from my little girl's school. There had been a gas leak and I was asked to come immediately to pick up my child. I jumped in my car and drove as fast as I dared to the school which is across the state line, but when I got there someone had taken my daughter home. I was frantic! By the time I found her and got back to my office you were here. The fact that you said you were going to the government frightened me and all I could think of was letting Mr. Near know right away. But I'm sorry! I shouldn't have done that."

The apology was accepted for I truly liked this young woman.

Then Belle began to quiz me as to what Carl's Public Health Service was all about.

"Did Mr. Lindstrom work for the State Public Health Service?"

"No, he was a United States Public Health Service commissioned officer."

"What did he do?"

"His first assignment was in South Dakota. He was the sanitary engineer on a health team whose goal it was to help the Indians of North and South Dakota, Nebraska, and Minnesota live a more healthful and sanitary life."

"What did he do specifically?"

"Well, as the sanitary engineer on the health team, part of Carl's job was to oversee the handling of food, the supply of water, and sanitation in the schools and hospitals on the Sioux and Chippewa reservations of those states. And, incidentally, as I stood at your door waiting for you to come back last Thursday I had a direct view of the Laurel dining room. There I watched a young aide fill the salad bar in preparation for dinner. She was using bare hands to fill the containers, and as she filled them she also used her hands to sample the food. Now, had I been a state inspector watching that procedure, Elm Grove would have had a citation. And if Carl's Indian sanitarian at the Rosebud Reservation hospital cafeteria had watched an employee make sandwiches without washing her hands and without the use of plastic gloves that hospital would have received demerits."

With these remarks I had obviously pointed out enough reasons for food handling citations at Elm Grove that Belle was no longer interested in what Carl did in the Dakotas. Discussion shifted to Tricia's and Nellie's trays.

"Do you think Tricia could drink apple juice or nectars if the grapefruit seems to bother her?"

"Absolutely! She has never resisted either one."

"I don't like to take Tricia completely off whole foods. This always seems so final and she should have the pleasure of chewing some of her food, I think. What if I have the beans and peas pureed? And if we give her some nice tender cubes of meat, like veal for example, do you think that would bother her?"

I told her I thought Tricia would enjoy that very much and I was sure that such substitutions would really take care of the problem. Then I asked if, after six months of feeding a patient I noticed a pattern of adverse reactions, did she not want to know about it because I was not a member of the staff? And when she came through the Ashley House dining room, as she sometimes did, and asked how everything was going, did she really want to know?

She replied, "I want any comment regarding any change you notice. If I am not here, just put a note under my door."

This did not sound like Near and Sharpe at my encounter with them yesterday. Here I was, not a staff member, sitting with the Elm Grove dietitian consulting with her—rather she with me—designing a diet for an Ashley House patient. Near and Sharpe would broil when told, and I was sure they would be. A one-on-one consultation regarding each and every patient, not by Belle and me, but by the nurses and Belle, should be an on-going requirement when need arises. Why procrastinate? Why always blame the kitchen?

How could Belle do her job without the nurses' comments regarding a patient's response to foods Belle prescribes, and any change which they notice? There must not be a set system of communication between the nurses and Belle in Elm Grove to insure this; lacking, too, a supervised follow-up of Belle's prescriptions. If there were, why would trays for Tricia and Nellie be brought into the dining room time and again for weeks on end with food they could not eat without chewing and chewing, choking, coughing and belching when these responses were directly observed by the nurses themselves or when brought to their attention? Why were Belle's prescriptions honored one day but not the next? Belle is a part-time employee. She performs her duties on Tuesdays and Thursdays. Isn't there anyone to supervise and follow through when she isn't there? Is there no supervision in the preparation of patients' trays to insure Belle's prescriptions are being carried out?

Patients in Ashley House are captives. They are not the persons they used to be, and they aren't able to cope with adversity all alone. As patients, they are unique individuals and should be treated as such. Patients should not be required to manage a 'mainstream' system of food preparation as Mr. Near supports—a system where, if they don't fit in, they must swim with the tide or sink. In a 'mainstream' system, when a patient is prescribed clear jello, and 'mainstream' prepares jello with nuts, then jello with nuts arrives on the patient's tray. It's jello, isn't it? In 'mainstream,' when a patient is prescribed broth, broth is skimmed off the top of the soup pot. What difference does it make if some beans, peas, or meat come with the broth? It's broth, isn't it? In Elm Grove there could not be any supervision of trays. If there were the supervisor was either indifferent, careless, or untrained. Mr. Near told me that Elm Grove had been taking care of Tricia and Nellie for years before I arrived on the scene and they were still alive. I could only conclude that Tricia and Nellie had been, and still were, great swimmers.

However, just being kept alive, which may be 'good enough' for Elm Grove, is not the 'excellence' that a patient in Ashley House should expect and receive. Surely, even now in their incapacitation and incompetence they still enjoy and recognize good food—its taste, its texture, and ease of assimilation. And along with that they surely appreciate a sprinkling of empathy and politeness. Otherwise, why would these poor old dears lay their trembling hands on mine when I gave them a pat, or in shaking voice say, "Thank you. Will you be here tomorrow?"

Mr. Near told me Elm Grove prepared 350,000 meals a year. Some of these were undoubtedly for the meals-on-wheels program in which Elm Grove participated. I can only surmise that Elm Grove can't do this and provide prescription feeding for the patients in Ashley House at the same time.

Curious about state rules regarding diets in nursing homes such as Ashley House, I asked Belle, "Does the state really say that a patient, regardless of height, weight, age, and activity, must be given 2000 calories a day? And if so, in what publication will I find these requirements? Carl would like to see this stated." Belle said that the state worried about those patients who may not get enough to eat and therefore established the rule. She added that no publication, as such, existed, but she had some information about this and she would get me a copy. I did not receive the information.

Then I asked, "If I fed Tricia systematically, first her juice, then upon finishing her soup thirty minutes later the dining room was cleared as was the custom, but I stayed thirty minutes more to feed her the entree, do I then, although Tricia likes dessert and needs some sugar, call it quits and send back her tray? And who checks on the preparation of that tray?"

Belle ignored the second question, but said that Tricia did not need all that liquid—juice, soup and milk. "Maybe she can be given some liquids in the afternoon. But feed as much fiber as you can." I recalled, but did not mention, that the charge nurse asked that Tricia be given all the liquids even if I could not feed anything else. This was contrary to what I was now hearing.

I thought, "If Tricia doesn't need all those liquids why did Belle prescribe them? If she didn't, how did they get on Tricia's tray?

Something is amiss! And if Belle decrees that fiber is more important than the liquids at dinner for Tricia but the nurse decrees the opposite, whose instructions do I follow? Who is in charge?"

My last question to Belle was, "Do you think I am being unreasonable? Do you think I am expecting too much from Elm Grove?" After hesitating, as though she were weighing her answer carefully, she replied, "No, Mrs. Lindstrom, I think you only want what I want—the best for the patients."

What a pleasant exchange this had been. Too bad Belle had been so upset last week over her personal problem—although I could certainly understand her concern for her child—that she had gone running to Mr. Near. Or was it too bad? If I had not had the encounter of the previous day when Near and Sharpe were so consumed with resentment toward me, I might never have known what this administration's true philosophy, human values, character and behavior really were.

I knew now that Carl and I could not live our lives at Elm Grove. When I was denied the right to advocate on behalf of Tricia and Nellie by the administrator and his associate, I knew, if Carl or I became an Ashley House patient in years to come, under this administration, no one would be permitted to advocate for us. I knew when the administration declared my dietary directive inadequate and ineffectual as far as Elm Grove was concerned, and when I was told that Elm Grove fed for the 'mainstream' and I obviously was not in the 'mainstream,' if ever I were permanently assigned to Ashley I could expect a 'mainstream' meal, heavy and citrus laden, each night. As an incompetent and without an advocate permitted, I would be at their mercy.

I also knew that my days of volunteering at Ashley House were numbered for I had no intention of sitting silently by and observing what I construed as unfair or unjust treatment of the elderly who could not speak for themselves. I intended, beginning this day, to record each day's experiences in a diary, for I had a premonition that one day, as a matter of principle, Carl and I would find ourselves as plaintiffs in a suit against Elm Grove to defend and claim not only our rights but the rights of all incompetent and incapacitated residents of all CCRCs. It seemed inevitable.

CHAPTER VI

"RETALIATION"

In addition to the area which houses those residents of Elm Grove who live in independent apartments and cottages, the Community has two additional levels of care both in separate wings located to the right of the main entrance. The upper level is for those residents in need of some personal care; the lower level, Ashley House, is the home of those in need of skilled care. The center of activity in Ashley House is a circular nurses' station out from which—north, south, east, and west—radiate long corridors. In three of these corridors one finds the private and semi-private rooms of the patients. The fourth corridor leads to the Ashley House lounge and activities/dining room. Opposite the nurses' station is a small, dark, dreary room which is used as a gathering room where the patients are assembled before and after being taken to the dining room for dinner. Its furniture consists of a few tables, some chairs, a cabinet which contains towels and bibs the patients wear at meal time, a hamper for soiled linens, and a poorly adjusted TV set which often blares while the patients are being assembled and to which no one seems to pay much attention. There are no windows to the outside and the room reminds me, because of its poor lighting, its atmosphere, and its isolation, of a dungeon; and for this reason I have dubbed it "The Dungeon". The corridor which runs between the nurses' station and the dining room carries the traffic of gerichairs and wheel chairs which are transporting the patients to and from the dining room at dinner time. The hustle and bustle can be observed when one is in "The Dungeon", through a bay of windows which line the wall on the side of the corridor.

Not long after my September 19 encounter with Near and Sharpe, it was to "The Dungeon" that I was banished by the charge nurse to feed a couple, Dr. and Mrs. Knight; and subsequently when Mrs. Knight died, to feed a recovering stroke victim who was taken directly from the Ashley dining room where she had eaten ever since being assigned to Ashley House seven months previously. No longer was I to see or have contact with my old friends, Tricia and Nellie, who remained in the Ashley dining room to be fed in a line-up of gerichairs by aides. In "The Dungeon", during the dinner hour, my charges and I were always alone— there never were any others except for a few times when "The Dungeon" was needed as an Ashley contingency.

I had not been dismissed as a volunteer by the administration; but it was obvious to me, as days went by, that I was to be kept out of the Ashley dining room as clearly and positively as could be done, and away from those whom I had fed, especially Tricia and Nellie. I was isolated even to the extent of being told I needn't carry my new charges' trays. This was a task which would have allowed me to go down the corridor to the entrance of Ashley's dining room where, nightly, carts from the kitchen loaded with trays were positioned. Previously, I had helped unload those trays and distribute them; but, by so doing now, I would have been privy to the contents of my old friends' trays. Yes! It had become quite obvious to me that the administration was shrewdly manipulating a plan to make me leave Ashley House voluntarily.

September 20, 1990 (From my diary)
    After my meeting with Belle this afternoon, I arrived at Ashley House for the dinner feeding. When Tricia's tray came it appeared

that I was on my way to solving her dietary needs. There was apple juice, the string beans were pureed, and the mashed potatoes were light and fluffy. There was no soup, and the veal, which was very tender, was cut in little cubes. Her dessert was a large dish of vanilla and chocolate pudding. Belle had done what she said she would and Tricia had no difficulties. About half way through the dinner, Belle came by and asked how everything was going. I told her, "Fine! Tricia hadn't choked or belched once!" But I questioned the piece of blueberry pie on Nellie's tray. I said that in the six months I had helped Nellie she hadn't had a piece of pie or cake and I wondered if someone had made a mistake. I had thought privately that perhaps Nellie was diabetic, but I dared not mention a medical opinion! "No. I put that on her chart tonight because she had lost two pounds last week." Note: I had been gone for a week, and when I came in this evening a private aide said to me, "Your two old friends really missed you last week! Those young aides just poked, poked, poked their food in their mouths for thirty minutes!" Was this the reason dear old Nellie lost two pounds in one week?

September 21, 1990

Tonight Tricia had apple juice, soup with bits of vegetables which clogged the straw, and "Spaghetti with Chunky Bits of Tomato." That was the description on the menu. The chunky bits were straight out of a can of tomatoes. Gourmet descriptions from the kitchen would be funny if they weren't so deceiving. There were carrots—some cooked well and Tricia could eat these, but some were so hard I couldn't cut them so I fed her only the soft ones. There were cherries for dessert and Tricia managed the first three, but on the fourth she choked violently just as the nurse came by. "Is Tricia having trouble?" And, I said that she did on some of the hard carrots and, apparently, on the cherry skins. Then the nurse said, "Don't feed her any more. She's had enough to eat. We don't want her to choke!" Contrary to the administration's edict I was still communicating with the nurses even if I were not staff, or a doctor. I still hadn't kept my mouth shut and Mr. Near, no doubt, will decide to do something about it.

September 22, 1990

Tricia tried to expel her drinking straw. I felt something was amiss and I asked, "Tricia, does your mouth hurt?" Although Tricia never talked to me, but always listened intently to everything I said, she would provide a "Yah!" or "No!" if asked a direct question. So when I asked if her mouth hurt and she said, "No!," I asked, "Do your teeth hurt?," and came a plaintive, "Yah!" Mr. Near had emphatically told me I was to offer no opinions and was not to practice medicine, so I was sticking my neck out when I called to the nurse across the room and told her to ask Tricia two questions: "Does your mouth hurt?" and "Do your teeth hurt?" Jane had never been too cordial to me and I wasn't sure, for a moment, that she would oblige; but when she asked the first question and Tricia began to yammer, Jane said crossly, "Stop that, Tricia! You can answer me properly!" Tricia stopped and said, "No!" Then Jane asked if her teeth hurt and Tricia answered, "Yah." I didn't say a word but I looked questioningly at the nurse. After glaring at me she said, "Well, I'll write in the report that Tricia should see the dentist." I thought, "Would I get barred from the Ashley dining room for countering Near's edict? Here I was practicing medicine and communicating with staff. I had been ordered by him to feed all that was on the tray, and to do, or say, nothing more.

September 23, 1990

Jane stopped by my table to inform me that the dentist had ordered Tylenol for Tricia. I hadn't asked her for this information—Jane volunteered. I didn't pursue Tricia's problem for Tylenol certainly wasn't the answer to a problem. But I couldn't help but wonder why I hadn't been thrown out of the dining room for offering an observation yesterday. However, I cautioned myself, "It is the weekend and it takes time to formulate plans, even for Elm Grove's administration!"

September 26, 1990

My favorite nurse, Bertha, was on duty tonight. She came by and whispered softly, "Tricia saw the dentist today." I knew immediately that my name had been in Jane's report, that it was I who had questioned Tricia's physical condition, else why would

Bertha have told me this? Instinctively I asked, "Did she have a problem?" Bertha hesitated before saying, "Yes." I didn't pursue the subject for I knew Bertha had already told me more than she was supposed to, and I had asked what was forbidden by the administration.

Tricia didn't really want the grape juice, but at least it wasn't grapefruit or tomato. Oh! But the entree! I fed Tricia and returned to my apartment angry to write a letter to Belle on behalf of Tricia who had been given a sorry dinner on top of a painful trip to the dentist. Belle had invited such correspondence, but I wondered if this, too, would be delivered urgently to the administration upon receipt of it. This is the note I slipped under Belle's door:

September 27, 1990

Dear Belle,

I'm registering a complaint on Tricia's behalf about last night's tray. On Sunday night I noticed that she was obviously in pain—something was wrong with her mouth. When I asked if her mouth hurt she said "No." When I asked if her teeth hurt she said, "Yes." I asked the nurse to repeat the questions and Jane got the same replies. Jane said that she'd tell the dentist.

On Monday Jane told me that the dentist was alerted and Tricia was given Tylenol.

Last night the nurse told me that Tricia had seen the dentist. When I asked if Tricia had a problem she said, "Yes." No details. But Tricia didn't want to open her mouth.

I coaxed her to drink the grape juice. But oh! the entree! A casserole of gummy—the only word for it—noodles about $5/8$ inches wide, six meatballs, and an ample serving of peas—undercooked and tough! There was a cup of soup with mushrooms and a strawberry dessert.

I fed her one third of the noodles and meatballs by chopping them as fine as I could but on the first teaspoon of peas she coughed so violently tears ran down her cheeks and moisture down her nose. I managed to extract a wad of fiber from her mouth, and when I asked if she wanted more peas I got an emphatic, "No!" The soup also was rejected. I can only guess it was too salty (I've tasted this brew in the coffee shop), and the salt burned the sore mouth. We got down the soft, custard-like strawberry dessert by spooning around the berries.

It was a sorry dinner for some old patient with a sore mouth. I can only wonder what happened to your instructions to the kitchen.

Sincerely,
Virginia K. Lindstrom

On October 9, 1990, Belle replied:

Dear Mrs. Lindstrom,
In response to your letter dated September 27, 1990 I investigated whether Tricia received the appropriate food for her dental condition. I met with the nursing staff and it was felt that Tricia's diet was appropriate. It was agreed that nursing would carefully monitor her intake and would report any necessary dietary modifications.

I wondered if Belle had prepared the correspondence she had signed.

September 27, 1990
Retaliation by the administration began this evening. And their plan to keep me out of the Ashley dining room, to make me voluntarily discontinue my services had been cleverly orchestrated. I had told Mr. Near on September 19 if he were to forbid me to return to Ashley House he'd have a lot of explaining to do to the residents who had been most complimentary about my volunteer work. But, I knew if he could force me out of my own volition there would be no fallout. He could tell the residents, "Mrs. Lindstrom just quit."

When I arrived at Ashley's holding room this evening, Merrie, the charge nurse, led me half way down a quiet corridor away from the nurses' station, away from the aides, and away from passing staff and residents. "Why the secrecy?" I wondered. Said Merrie, "The other night I was on the patio outside the dining room taking my cigarette break, and everyone had gone from Ashley's dining room except, you, Tricia, and Nellie when Tricia began to cough." I recalled, silently, that Tricia did not cough when she was alone with me the other night—last Friday when she choked on the cherry skin, or last night when she choked on the tough old peas, Tricia and I were in the dining room when all the patients, nurses, and aides were there. Merrie was concocting this story! I listened curiously as she continued, "And I thought that if Tricia should choke when you were in the dining room alone it could be tragic." What was she leading to? Tragic? Hadn't Marcie Sharpe, herself, told me that all I had to do was yell, "Help!" and nurses would be there in seconds?

Merrie was trying hard to justify what she was about to do, and was not doing a very convincing job although I'm sure she thought she was doing just fine. "So," she continued, "I have decided to assign an aide to feed Nellie and Tricia in the dining room, and I'm putting Dr. and Mrs. Knight—Hope—in the little room off the nurses' station, and you can feed Hope there. She's easy to feed—has all pureed foods—and if she begins to choke the nurse right there at the station will be able to help. Dr. Knight can feed himself but you can keep him company." Thus, I was surreptitiously removed from the Ashley dining room and from Nellie and Tricia, and I was relegated to "The Dungeon"—Merrie's "that little room off the nurses' station". Retaliation by the administration had begun. I was to carry on in isolation. I wondered, "If it is necessary to have a nurses' station in close proximity for quick response in an emergency when I am alone with my charges, why couldn't I continue to feed Nellie and Tricia in "The Dungeon"? Why did I have to be divorced from them?" Perhaps Near and Sharpe hoped that tonight they could savor the victory of their ingenious plan. Perhaps that was the reason for my being taken halfway down the corridor before the news was broken. Perhaps they had anticipated a scene and were removing me from aides, patients, and residents who had been visiting in the rooms and were now on their way to the main dining room upstairs. If that were the case, I disappointed them, for without a word to Merrie I left her and walked to "The Dungeon" to feed my new charges.

When I walked in, the round table in "The Dungeon" had already been arranged by some member of the staff for the Knights and me. My chair had been placed so that my back was to the corridor which was visible through the bay of windows. Dr. Knight and Hope were already waiting, her wheelchair to my right and he across the table from her. Obviously I was not even to be permitted a sight of the corridor, to smile and wave to my old friends who had each evening greeted me with smiles and with tight handclasps. And when, during feeding Hope, I could hear the phone ring ten times I could not see whether the nurse who was to assist me if I needed help was just ignoring the ringing or whether she actually sat there. I resolved that tomorrow night I would arrange the seating at this table so that I would be able to watch the Ashley world go by.

Hope was as easy to feed as Merrie had said. I finished the task in thirty minutes and asked a nurse passing by if there were someone else I could help. I received a sharp, "No! You're only supposed to be here thirty minutes!" Retaliation had been hard hitting and I went out into the stairwell and cried.

I cried because I had been forced to lie to my old friend, Nellie. Each night, when I had finished feeding Nellie and Tricia I would say, "Good night, Nellie, I'll see you tomorrow." Sometimes, as I have said, Nellie was very alert and would answer, "Good night and thanks." Some nights she would come into the dining room grumpy and demanding, and I would repeat my good nights several times before she answered. Tricia, on the other hand, never answered but I always patted her gently on the hand and said softly, "Good night, Tricia, I'll see you tomorrow." At my touch Tricia would tremble and I had a feeling that mine was the only gentle voice she heard all day. Not so with Nellie. The nurses seemed to make a great fuss over "Aunt Nellie". She came to the dining room often with make-up on her cheeks and ribbons in her hair.

The previous night, when I said good night, Nellie refused to answer. Several times I bade her good night and finally said, "Nellie, aren't you going to say good night to me?" Nellie looked at me and blurted out, "Are you going out West again?" I can only surmise that Nellie had heard someone say the week before, when I was gone, that I had a visitor from the West. In her addled mind I had gone out West. Hence the question. I assured her that I was not going West again, and then she asked childlike, "Will you be here tomorrow?" I told her wild horses couldn't keep me away. With that she smiled very sweetly and said, "Then good night and thank you." But it wasn't a wild horse that kept me away—it was Mr. Near and Ms. Sharpe. Little comfort, that, as I stood in the stairwell and cried.

At this point I must introduce my new charges: Dr. Knight, 90, and Hope, his wife, aged 88. Since I first began feeding Nellie and Tricia, and seemingly before, I had observed that nightly a table was set up by staff for the Knights in Ashley's lounge just outside, but in close proximity to, the dining room. There they sat alone while Dr. Knight fed Hope first, then bolted his own food in five or ten minutes, rose, and pushed Hope's wheelchair out of the lounge and down the corridor. I had felt sorry for Dr. Knight as I observed them night after night, for his hand trembled and he seemed to spill as much food as he fed to his wife.

Only once did I see a deviation from this pattern. Several weeks prior to their being transferred from the lounge to "The Dungeon" with me, a daughter and grandson came to visit. That night their table was moved to the middle of Ashley's dining room next to Nellie's, Tricia's, and my table, and set for four. Before the meal was finished, the daughter rose and came back to our table to introduce herself to me. She asked if I were a resident of Elm Grove and if I did this often. When I told her that I was here almost nightly she said, "God bless you!" I thanked her and assured her He already had.

The second evening in "The Dungeon" I rearranged the seating at the Knights' table so that I sat facing the corridor and could wave to old patients and friends as they were wheeled past the window, who looked in, smiled, and waved in turn. Tonight, if the phone rang, I could see whether or not a nurse really sat behind the desk, but was ignoring the caller.

As I fed Hope, I kept up a running, albeit almost a one-sided conversation with Dr. Knight. Certainly he was old and undoubtedly forgetful but he was following the conversation intently, and he quit gobbling his food. I recounted for him what I thought were interesting tidbits about Carl's and my twenty years in the West. I told him about renting a very beautiful condo for the summer in Deer Valley which, I said, was about twenty-five miles east of Salt Lake City. I did not mention the state. I described other rentals at Glacier and Steamboat Springs. When I finished he asked, "But the one in Utah was the nicest, wasn't it?" Oh, yes! Beside needing help in feeding Hope, Dr. Knight was much in need of conversation.

When Hope's tray was empty I asked, "May I have dinner with you tomorrow night?" And this dear old man said most graciously, "It will be our pleasure! This was most fascinating!"

September 29, 1990

It was a beautiful, sunny, warm autumn day—the kind that would make anyone who loves the outdoors want to be out enjoying every last minute of a fast fading summer.

When I arrived at "The Dungeon" there was no sign of the Knights, nor of food. I spread the cloth on the table and arranged the chairs so that I would be facing the corridor to wave to friends as they were wheeled by. Since my new charges hadn't appeared I wandered toward the nurses' station to see if the Knights were being brought down the hall from their room. The girl on duty behind the desk, who incidentally was not a nurse, was frantic. Quivering with excitement, she asked, "Aren't you the person who fed Hope and Dr. Knight last evening?"

"Yes. And the night before."

"Oh! He's trying to break out! He's been trying all afternoon! Can you help us?"

Could *I* help *them*? Here was staff asking for help from me when the administrator had told me last week that I could feed the patients assigned to me, but that was all—just feed! However, I asked what she meant by trying to break out. I was told that Dr. Knight was trying to leave—that he was at the far end of the corridor trying to break out. "Please! Can you help us?"

I said, "I'll try," and I walked down the corridor. There at the closed door which led to the beautiful autumn woods and behind Hope's chair stood Dr. Knight, confronted by one of the aides. He was very angry and Hope reflected his mood, for her beautiful blue eyes, which were usually so calm and peaceful, were ablaze with anger. I could only assume that Dr. Knight had promised her a ride in the autumn sunshine. The aide was trying to explain that if he opened the door an alarm would go off. He turned pathetically to me and asked, "Is she telling the truth?" I said that she was, and then I asked, "Dr. Knight, don't you remember that we had a dinner engagement tonight? I was going to tell you about some of Carl's and my adventures in the Dakotas where Carl was working with the Sioux Indians. And I brought along a piece of quill work which I thought you might like to examine." With that, I pulled the quill bracelet from my pocket and distracted him. Dr. Knight turned around pushing Hope in her wheelchair and headed for our private dining room in "The Dungeon".

With my chair facing the corridor I could see my old friend, Tricia, sitting in her gerichair outside the door of "The Dungeon". It was 5:10 P.M. when an aide pushed her down the corridor, past the bay of windows, and it was 5:25 P.M. when she was trundled back again and left by the door. Some aide had fed Tricia in fifteen minutes.

The Knights' trays were brought into "The Dungeon" and Dr. Knight ate as though he were starved. Tonight he gobbled his food in ten minutes. Having finished, he sat quietly in his chair until I finished feeding Hope, and then he took the handles of her wheelchair and was off! I cleared the table, threw the cloth in the hamper, and pushed the chairs back against the wall. When I came out of "The Dungeon" the same distraught employee said, "He's trying again! Will you help us?"

I wanted to say, "Tough! Maybe he'll make it this time. The poor old man just wants a breath of fresh air." But I restrained the impulse and went to see if I could distract him once more.

This time he was trying the door that led to the Maintenance Department. I told him where the door went, what was on the other side, and I said, "I'll bet you're trying to take Hope to the sun parlor to watch the sunset, aren't you?" He said that was where he thought he was going. As I turned him around I told him I'd show him the way, but Drusilla intervened. Did she take him to the sun parlor or was he taken to his room to be put to bed?

September 30, 1990

Sunday dinners at Elm Grove are served at noon, the evening meal is a light supper. Hope's tray contained the ordered pureed food. Dr. Knight's tray consisted of grape juice, soup, a turkey sandwich, a bowl of cooked spinach, fruit cocktail, and a glass of tea. He quickly gobbled everything except the spinach, took the lid off the container, sampled it, put the lid back on. Several times he went through this ritual, taking just a small spoonful each time until I said,

"You don't like spinach, do you, Dr. Knight?"

"No ma'am."

"Do you make out your menu or is it made out by someone for you?"

"I guess someone makes it out for me."

"Why don't you tell the nurse that you don't like spinach and that you'd much rather have a vegetable you can eat?"

"Oh! I don't think I'm allowed to do that!"

"Sometimes the dietitian comes around on Tuesdays or Thursday, and sometimes she asks me how things are going. When she asks that the next time may I tell her that you don't like spinach?"

"That would be fantastic!"

But I wondered, "Will it do any good?"

October 4, 1990

Tassie, a patient in Ashley House whom I had enjoyed helping, on the way to the Ashley dining room reached out her hand to catch mine and said, "We miss you!" I told her that I missed them, too, but I was asked to help Hope in the TV room.

"I know," she said. "I saw you in there."

Hope's dinner consisted of mashed potatoes covered with a thick layer of heavy brown gravy. There was no room for the pat of butter that always came with her potatoes. She also had pureed roast beef drowned in the same thick gravy. Dr. Knight had a piece of fish which I could smell across the table.

The phone at the desk rang ten times. This time I could see there was no one there to answer. So much for someone being there to help me.

October 5, 1990

I arrived at "The Dungeon" at 4:45 P.M. It was empty except for the Knights. But instead of seating them at the round table in the center of the room as had been customary, they had been seated by staff at a table at the far end of the room against the windowless wall. Hope sat at one side of the table next to the blank wall. Dr. Knight sat with head bowed directly opposite. This would have necessitated my facing the windowless wall and not the bay of windows which would allow me to view the corridor.

I said, "Let's move to the round table in the center of the room, shall we? We don't want to look at that dreary wall, do we, Hope?" And I wheeled her chair to the round table, placed a chair to her left for Dr. Knight, and seated myself at Hope's right so I had a view of the corridor. Dr. Knight did not move from the back table; his head remained bowed.

At 4:55 P.M. an aide brought in Hope's tray, and followed in a few minutes with Dr. Knight's tray which she proceeded to take to the back table where the old man still sat with head bowed. I asked her if she couldn't move Dr. Knight to the table where Hope and I were sitting since he liked to eat with his wife. She didn't appear to be pleased, but she moved him sullenly. I was sure the aide would put me on report but I smilingly said to Dr. Knight, "You don't want to eat alone, do you, Dr. Knight?" and he assured me that he didn't.

At exactly 5:20 P.M. I saw my old friend, Nellie, being trundled back from the dining room to her room. And in five minutes Tricia, in her gerichair, was brought into "The Dungeon". These two old dears who had enjoyed an hour and fifteen minutes of socializing and dinner with me for almost six months had been stuffed—or not—in 20 minutes.

Tricia sat there trembling, for the tape recorder had been turned on so loudly that Dr. Knight and I couldn't talk across the table. After feeding Hope, I turned off the tape recorder, went over to Tricia who sat trembling in her gerichair, spoke gently to her and patted her hand. Again as she had done the other night, she straightened at the sound of my voice and her thin old fingers clutched my hand. I left with tears in my eyes.

October 6, 1990

Today the electricity was out all over Elm Grove from eight this morning until four this afternoon while the lines were being checked. Elm Grove's main dining room was closed, but at 4:45 P.M. Ashley House was to have its usual dinner hour. Apparently there was a shortage of aides for, when I arrived, I found that all Ashley patients had been ushered into "The Dungeon" for the evening meal. Hope had been seated at a table almost directly behind the bay of windows which overlooked the corridor. Nellie, in a wheelchair, had been positioned to Hope's left with barely enough room for my chair between them. An aide attempted to seat a patient across the table from Hope since there was no room anywhere else, for six gerichairs lined the wall to Hope's right with barely enough room for aides to stand to feed the patients. I stopped the aide saying that Dr. Knight would sit there since he always sat with his wife at dinner. There I was ordering staff.

Tricia was number one in the row of gerichairs lined up against the wall. Apparently her mouth was still bothering her for drool oozed out the corner.

I watched the trays being brought in with fascination. Nellie's tray, which was typical, consisted of two glasses of nectar, a bowl of cottage cheese, an ice cream scoop of egg salad, a large jello salad with fruit cocktail, a package of crackers, two celery sticks, a long thin slice of carrot, about one-half cup of green and red grapes, two large cookies, a cup of minestrone soup, and a carton of milk. The tray could hardly hold it all. Could aides be sued by the state for not feeding all of this to the patients?

But good grief! Tricia had exactly the same foods on her tray! Where's the pureed food? It will be interesting to see the aide feed her the celery sticks.

Dr. Knight's tray consisted of a sandwich, juice, tea, two cookies, and a green banana which, if I had taken it to my apartment and put it in a ripening bowl, would still have been green in a week. The aide put the tray in front of him and scurried off. As I fed Hope I could see him devour the sandwich hungrily. He ate his soup, drank his juice, gobbled his cookies. Then he picked up that hard, green banana and tugged at the end of it. Three times he picked it up, looked at it, fingered the end, and then put it down. Authorized or not, I could watch this no longer and I spoke to the aide to my right who was feeding a gerichair-patient and carrying on an animated conversation about a square dance with two other aides and asked if she couldn't find a banana which Dr. Knight could eat. Fliply she replied, "It is a little green, isn't it?" Taking it away she returned with a ripe one. Dr. Knight would have eaten that green banana if he could have removed the peel. In my anger over the lack of supervision and common sense in preparing the old doctor's tray,

I didn't stop to worry about the demerits I was accumulating this evening.

Nor was this the end of my unauthorized behavior. Nellie kept trying to pull her tray onto her lap—something Nellie always does—and I kept pushing it back toward the center of the table as I fed Hope her pureed foods. Asking Nellie to be patient was a waste of breathe for Nellie was hungry. Finally I realized no one was coming, so I fed Nellie, too, between teaspoons of food for Hope and glances in Dr. Knight's direction. A nurse came by and I said, "I know I'm only authorized to feed Hope, but Nellie was getting impatient and no one offered to help her, so I took it upon myself to feed her too." The nurse said, "I appreciate your taking the initiative." But would Near and Sharpe appreciate my taking the initiative? They will be told about it, I'm sure.

Nellie would not eat the celery or carrot sticks. I had put each in her hand so that she could feed on these herself while I finished feeding Hope, but she laid each back on the table saying about the celery, "It isn't done!"

Oh! If only I could have helped poor Tricia sitting in that gerichair in the line-up against the wall. I heard her choke and wondered what the aide had tried to force on her. The celery? The carrots? The grapes?

This letter, in part, went under the dietitian's door the next morning.

October 7, 1990

Dear Belle,

As you undoubtedly know I no longer feed Tricia and Nellie in the Ashley dining room. Following my last note to you (on September 27) in which I had the temerity to criticize the tray sent to Tricia who had a sore mouth and a session with the dentist I was assigned to Hope and Dr. Knight—not in the dining room but in that dreary little room off the nurses' station. Hence, I have had no access to the Ashley dining room or my old friends until last night when there was an obvious shortage of staff and all the patients were herded into the Knights' dining area.

Nellie's tray was placed in front of her, Hope's pureed food was delivered and Dr. Knight's tray was set before him. And as I fed Hope and Nellie also, I observed Dr. Knight. His tray included a banana so green and hard that had I taken it to my apartment and put it in a ripening dish it would not have been edible until next Saturday.

Now I've had it made perfectly clear that the administration appreciates my feeding patients so long as that is all I do. I am to offer no opinions or criticisms, but when I could not stand the sight of that old man wanting that banana and not being able to eat it, edict or not, I called an aide over and told her I'd like her to get Dr. Knight a banana he could eat. She said, "It is a little green, isn't it? I'll see what I can do." And in a few minutes she was back with a ripe fruit which he quickly ate.

My question: since a member of the staff prepared that tray, since a member of the staff inspected that tray, since a member of the staff put that try in front of that old man, who on the staff cared one whit as to whether or not Dr. Knight could eat and ingest the potassium you undoubtedly felt he needed on his supper tray?

Sincerely,
Virginia K. Lindstrom

I received this reply from Belle concerning the green banana on October 9, 1990.

Dear Mrs. Lindstrom,

In response to your letter dated October 7, 1990, it was unfortunate that Dr. Knight received a green banana. Staff has been spoken to about this incident. I was happy to hear that staff was able to remedy the situation and provide the patient with a good banana.

Sincerely,
Belle

Since a copy of her reply undoubtedly went to Mr. Near and Miss Sharpe I presume that this was the best Belle could do.

October 30, 1990

We bought a car this P.M. and the paper work took all afternoon, so I was fifteen minutes late arriving at Ashley House. The lights were out in "The Dungeon", but the two elderly patients sitting in the room in the dark were not the Knights so I asked a nurse passing by where the Knights were after explaining why I was fifteen minutes late. She curtly said, "In the main dining room!" I stood there for approximately thirty seconds not saying a word for I had apologized, and finally, irritated, she said, "You can ask Merrie what you can do. She's down there!" Was there any doubt that I was not supposed to go near the dining room?

Merrie stood just outside the dining room mixing medicines at her cart. Again I offered my apology for being fifteen minutes late, but many times dinner trays were that late in coming down from the kitchen. She hesitated, as though trying to decide whether or not I could come into the dining room. I was absolutely certain at that point, by her actions and by her expression, that she had been told to keep me out. But there, no more than four feet in front of us, at the very first round table were Meg, Dr. Fry, Dr. Knight, and Hope. Dr. Knight was eating as were the other two, but Hope was sitting there with her untouched tray in front of her and no one standing by to feed her. Merrie knew I saw this. Finally she said, "Well, you can feed Hope here in the dining room. I'll get you a chair." I surmised that I was not even to walk through this room for on many an evening I had carried my own chair as well as the trays to the table to sit between Tricia and Nellie.

The chair was placed between the Knights which let me face directly the line of gerichairs against the wall. And there, in front of me, not more than five feet away, sat my old friend, Tricia, slumped over the side of her chair and trembling like an aspen. In front of her was her tray. I couldn't determine the contents of the tureen nor see the dessert, but I could see a small glass of tomato juice, half full. Did she drink it or had it been spilled in the conveyor on the way down from the kitchen? In addition, there was her carton of milk unopened. The clock on the wall said 5:10 P.M. If she had been brought in at the normal time she had been here for twenty-five minutes.

About 5:15 P.M. Merrie straightened Tricia in her chair. Pillows, which had been made by a resident to help Tricia sit upright in her chair, were not evident. An aide, who had been feeding a patient down the line, strolled back to Tricia and shoved a huge spoonful of food into Tricia's mouth. Tricia chewed and chewed as she had for me, but before she could swallow another huge spoonful was shoveled in. About 5:30 P.M. the milk carton was opened and poured into her glass. No straw for this aide! From time to time she would tilt Tricia's head back against her chair and force the milk in to wash down the food Tricia had pouched in either cheek. Once Tricia choked and the aide walked away and down the line to feed another patient. When Tricia stopped coughing the aide returned to the shoveling of food and forcing of milk.

Hope had finished her meal but I was determined to stay for I probably would never have another opportunity to get in this dining room. Would all the liquids be fed to Tricia as Merrie had said should be? So I walked across the room to chat with Mollie— Mollie with the beautiful, pleading brown eyes—and I positioned myself to watch Tricia and the aide. At 5:50 P.M. all the milk had not been consumed for the carton would have provided a second glass the size of the one on the tray. I couldn't tell whether or not Tricia had been fed the entire entree and dessert but the tray was whipped away when the dining room was cleared. The half glass of tomato juice was placed before her on the gerichair tray. The aide returned in a few minutes and tried to force the juice down, but Tricia resisted so the juice was taken away too. I wanted to accost that aide and tell her that was not the way to treat my old friend!

On the way back to my apartment I recalled Near's telling me that they had taken care of Tricia for seven years before I came into her life—that they didn't need my help. They may not have needed it but certainly Tricia did. At least for the six months of the past seven and a half years the poor dear had been treated like a human being. And I silently prayed as I walked along that nothing would happen to Carl and me before we were able to leave Elm Grove which would necessitate our occupying a chair beside Tricia or Nellie in Ashley House.

October 31, 1990

Today was Halloween and I took Dr. Knight some chocolate witches for I knew he was very fond of chocolate. I asked Bertha, my favorite nurse, if I were allowed to give him this treat after he had eaten and she said, "Of course!"

He had been brought to the table in his pajamas. The aide told me he had tried to escape three times today. Was that the reason he came to dinner in pj's?

November 5, 1990

Dr. Knight wasn't at the table when I got there but he was brought in very shortly thereafter by an aide who looked very disgusted. As he sat across the table from me, his eyes twinkled and he was as merry as a schoolboy who had just festooned the principal's front yard with toilet tissue on Halloween. He clapped his hands and exclaimed, "Oh! I've just had a magnificent adventure!" His delight was so evident I encouraged him to tell me about it.

"I got outside!"

"How did you manage that?" I prodded.

"Well I just went out through that door into the garden and there wasn't anyone around and I went down to the road. (This from a man who is supposed to be senile. Forgetful, yes. Senile, no—for he described the route he had taken perfectly) I crossed to the other side of the road and followed along until I saw some garages down over the hill. And I went down to see if I could find someone because I was getting tired and I hadn't taken my walker. There was no one there but luckily just then a truck came along. I didn't know the driver, but apparently he knew me, for he said, "Dr. Knight, wouldn't you like a lift?" And I said, "Oh yes!" I was getting really tired and a little worried because I didn't see anyone, and that was a big hill I had come down. "But," said Dr. Knight in conclusion, "it was a great adventure and it was such a nice day!"

The charge nurse came in just then, turned her back on Dr. Knight and in a stage whisper said to me, "We've had trouble with Dr. Knight today so if you see him try to leave call me immediately!" Why do these nurses assume that elderly people like Dr. Knight are completely unaware? Her back was turned to him but he had been watching and listening closely. As she walked away I winked at him, and he silently clapped his hands. For a week he had been trying to get outside and had finally made it. He had had a great adventure and he had shared it with his friend.

He ate his dinner slowly—taking forty minutes to finish, not in the five or ten as he had done when I first began helping the Knights.

November 6, 1990

Today I saw Dr. Leo, Elm Grove's medical director, in spite of Mr. Near's pronouncement, "You may not consult with Dr. Leo! He's a busy man! His time is money!"

In October, Dr. Lillie, a gastroenterologist, to whom Dr. Leo had referred me, advised surgery sometime in the future. The surgery wasn't urgent, but the symptoms were there—the election was mine. This conference with Dr. Lillie gave me the opportunity to describe in detail the philosophy and stance of Elm Grove's administration concerning my dietary directive and my future health care. Dr. Lillie found it shocking that I might not talk with Dr. Leo because he was a busy man and his time was money. Emphatically rejecting such behavior, Dr. Lillie said, "I'll ask Dr. Leo to see you concerning my recommendations and once in the office you can consult with him about your directive. I'll prepare a letter as a follow-up on my services, and I'll also advise him of my recommendations for your dietary restrictions and regimen." Upon receipt of Dr. Lillie's correspondence, Dr. Leo set up an appointment with me for an office visit.

Carl accompanied me to Dr. Leo's office. There would be no more meetings with the Elm Grove hierarchy by myself. I took along my notarized dietary directive to request Dr. Leo to place it in my medical file which he maintained.

Upon entering the office, I thanked the doctor for seeing me, for referring me to Dr. Lillie, and I expressed appreciation for Dr. Lillie's prescribed diet and regimen—it had bolstered my confidence in what I was, and had been, following.

When I presented my notarized dietary directive to Dr. Leo and asked that it be placed in my medical file, he glanced at it and said, "I already have that in your record." Upon my, "You couldn't have," he proceeded to extract it as proof. The document that had been inserted in my medical file was a copy of my notarized directive, for I still had in my possession all three of the originals which included the one I had snatched from Marcie Sharpe at our September meeting. This copy was the one, or a duplicate, that the notary public had made over my objections. How many copies were circulating throughout Elm Grove? Until now, I was under the impression that notarization was a private matter—a legal one.

Dr. Leo, after a bit of fanfare in reinserting the copy, and adding to it the original which I had just handed him, said, without inspecting its contents, that my directive should have included the foods I wanted. I knew, at that moment, that Marcie Sharpe had conferred with the doctor, for she had also used that same word, 'wanted,' when she denounced my directive as unworthy of consideration. If Dr. Leo, Ms. Sharpe, and Mr. Near considered my directive ineffectual, why did Dr. Leo now place my original in my medical file? If it were of no use, why hadn't one of these custodians of my health care offered to assist me in the preparation of a directive acceptable to them since they knew of my concern. Governmental statutes and policies of the Board of Directors express the rights of patients to be involved in the planning of their total care and to establish advanced directives. But morally, in any caring Community, this should be honored without the enforcement of law.

Days later, someone placed a copy of my notarized addendum to my Living Will in my mailbox marked, "For your file". Was this the copy that Dr. Leo had produced at our meeting? Or was this yet another copy of the copy placed there by the Social Service Director? Or had Marcie Sharpe, after her anger abated, decided that she had wrongfully rejected my attempt to add an addendum to my Living Will and was attempting, in a clumsy way, to rectify her mistake?

Dr. Leo is a contractual physician and Marcie Sharpe approves all contracts. It appeared to me that Dr. Leo wasn't about to place his position in jeopardy. His patronizing manner and agreement with Marcie Sharpe that my directive was incomplete angered me. He must have seen the fire in my eyes when I said, "If ever I am so unfortunate as to end up in Ashley House just see to it that I am given none of the negatives on that list!"

But with this, I knew for certain that I would be fed 'mainstream' in Ashley House, just as Near and Sharpe decreed, if ever I were not able to fend for myself and that Dr. Leo's filing of my directive in my medical file was just a gesture to placate me. Dr. Leo had just shattered my hopes that he would ever be my advocate.

Before I left, however, I quizzed Dr. Leo about his thoughts concerning my right to advocate for Tricia and Nellie, to complain if necessary, and to offer suggestions or criticisms to Mr. Near and Ms. Sharpe—or any member of the staff at Elm Grove—concerning mistreatment, as I saw it, in the feeding of patients in Ashley House. He already knew, I was sure, of Marcie Sharpe's and Near's mandate, that if I wanted to continue as a volunteer I must feed the patients silently. He undoubtedly had been told of my resentment and disobedience to that edict, for Dr. Leo said, "Only the patient has the right."

Upon my response that the patients in Ashley House were incapacitated, for the most part, and incompetent and unable to speak for themselves and that governmental statutes give all advocates, including me, the right to speak for them, Dr. Leo said, "I think you should go back and talk with Mr. Near again." My furious reply, "I shall never set foot in that office again!" brought an unexpected, "You're wise! You'll probably live longer that way."

Dr. Lillie had helped me gain admittance to Dr. Leo's office. I had come to consult with Elm Grove's resident physician about my future health care. The professional advice I received about that matter—and for which I was billed—was to stay away from Sharpe and Near if I hoped to live longer. Could this be a warning if we continued to live in Elm Grove? An omen?

November 7, 1990

Hope was lying on a lambswool cover on a gerichair when I came in tonight. Her cheeks were two bright red splotches—undoubtedly from fever—and her eyes were glazed. I sought out Bertha and said, "I don't think I'm going to get Hope to eat very much tonight."

Bertha replied with a sad smile, "I don't think you will either." I told Dr. Knight the same thing since he always came over to see if Hope had eaten her whole dinner, and my dear old friend said, "You'll be able to feed her more than I could," and after a hesitation, "and more than those girls could!" (Referring to the young aides.)

I managed all of her liquids and some pureed apricots until she weakly said, "No more."

November 8, 1990

Merrie told me Hope would not be in for dinner tonight. "We're losing her," she said. I asked if there were someone else I could help and she said, "I'd like you to keep Dr. Knight company. I don't know whether he knows what's going on." He knew! He told me about his children while he took thirty-six minutes to eat his dinner—a far cry from the five minutes of just a month ago.

November 9, 1990

Upon arriving at "The Dungeon" I saw that the round table was in the middle of the room, but there were no chairs around it. Dr. Knight was sitting in one of the chairs next to the nurses' station. An aide was sitting beside him and talking earnestly to him.

A nurse came by and said, "Did you know Hope had died? And their daughter is here?"

I said, "Yes", to both questions, and said that I only intended to set up the table for them. I had no intention of intruding on their grief.

When the aide left, I sat down beside Dr. Knight, and putting my hand on his, I said, "Dr. Knight, we're all going to miss Hope." His reply was, "Indeed we are! But that's life!"

The answer surprised me. There was no tear in the voice, no resignation. Emboldened, I said, "You're right, Dr. Knight. I told the doctor not long ago that we all come into this world owing a life, and our debt isn't paid until we give up that life."

He said, "That's a fantastic philosophy! What did the doctor say?"

I told him that the doctor didn't say anything, but he looked a little startled.

Then this dear old man said, "I often wonder just how long I'll be given. I wouldn't mind having another ten years."

I said that I hoped he'd get them, and if I were around for another ten years I'd come to visit him. And we both laughed, at which the red-haired nurse behind the nurses' station looked up disapprovingly as though we were being disrespectful.

When his daughter came by I told her I had their table set up in the adjoining room. She was going to the coffee shop to pick up a tray, and she told her father not to eat fast—she didn't want to eat alone. I informed her that he was overcoming that habit; that when I first began to feed her mother he finished his dinner in five or ten minutes, but during these past few weeks, with conversation, we were stretching it out to thirty minutes or more.

When she returned, but before I left, I said, "Before you go home please visit the dietitian and tell her there is one food your father doesn't like. I can't tell her but you can."

She wanted me to tell her what it was, but I turned to Dr. Knight and said, "You tell her!" With absolutely no prompting this old man, who is considered quite incompetent, replied quickly, "Spinach!"

I laughed and said, "That's it! He doesn't like it cooked and he doesn't like it raw. Tell the dietitian that."

Within weeks Dr. Knight joined his beloved wife.

November 10, 1990

When I arrived at "The Dungeon", a single overhead light was on above the table in the middle of the room. All of the patients had been taken to the main dining room except for one patient who was sitting in a gerichair at that table. I couldn't see who she was for her back was to the bay of windows, but I knew, instinctively, that this lone person had been left for me. Drusilla was the nurse in charge and when I asked, "Whom shall I help tonight?" she paused, as though making a weighty decision and then said, "Well-l-l, Evelyn is still in there. You might feed her there, for she would benefit from a little conversation with her dinner." I wanted to say, "Wouldn't they all, Drusilla?"

I positioned my chair beside Evelyn's and her first comment was, "Where did everyone go? Why did they leave me here all by myself?" I wondered, "How long has she been sitting here all alone waiting for someone to help her?"

I said that the others had gone to the dining room and then she wanted to know why they hadn't taken her too. I explained that I knew that since she had been ill she was having a hard time feeding herself and I was going to help her learn how to do that more easily. But the next question should have been answered by the administrator or his associate for she asked, "Why can't you help feed me in the dining room?"

I cut Evelyn's food in small pieces, put the pieces on her spoon, placed the spoon in her hand, and then helped her guide it to her mouth. Long before we were finished the aides began returning patients from the dining room, lining some of the chairs against the wall in the hall, wheeling others into the room where we sat. Again Evelyn wanted to know where these people had been and why they were coming in here now. And again, "Why didn't we go to the dining room?"

I returned to the apartment to tell Carl about my new assignment, about the put-up job, and about incapacitated Evelyn's reaction. I was incensed over this, although I knew when I had been shuttled into "The Dungeon" more than a month ago, that I had been restricted from Ashley's dining room. Tomorrow night shall be my last night as a volunteer.

November 11, 1990

Ironic that on Armistice Day I would begin my war against Elm Grove. I sat in an alcove near the kitchen where I had a direct view of dinner trays being taken to the elevator so that they could be transported to the ground floor. I waited until all the trays were down and the young man who transported them returned. By then I knew that all the patients should have been wheeled into the Ashley dining room. Then I slowly descended the stairs that led to the corridor opposite "The Dungeon". And there, sitting in "The Dungeon" alone, again, was Evelyn. I didn't go in to speak to her, but instead I marched down the hall where Drusilla was helping aides lift trays out of the dolly. I said very bruskly to her, "Please send someone to bring Evelyn to the dining room for dinner. It's unfair to segregate Evelyn because you have to segregate Virginia Lindstrom!" And she replied, "All right. Whatever." I repeated the 'whatever' with a firm shake of the head, turned, and walked into the waiting elevator.

Back at the apartment I told Carl that my volunteering at Ashley House was over. We spent the evening assessing our situation, and it was a precarious one. We knew exactly where we stood with the administration in this Life Care Community but it was a matter of principle that they should not be allowed to get away with this. "Elm Grove will sue you!" had undoubtedly silenced others but Robert Near and Marcie Sharpe had finally tried to clone the wrong little, old lady!

CHAPTER VII

"DESTINY"

Following is an extract from Elm Grove's contractual Agreement, *Decisions Involving Permanent Transfer from the Living Accommodations:* "All decisions relating to permanent transfer from the resident's living accommodations to a skilled nursing or personal care facility, an appropriate special service facility, or hospital, are made by an Interdisciplinary Committee. The Committee consists of at least the Medical Director, the Administrator, representatives of the Nursing Staff, the Social Services Staff, and a member of the Board of Directors of the Community. Written recommendation is initiated by a Community Physician or the Administrator. A decision of the Interdisciplinary Committee is binding."

Thus, the Interdisciplinary Committee is a child of the agreement. But, the agreement merely authorizes its existence, defines its minimal membership, and expresses its objectives. Promulgation, that is, the explicit design of the membership of the Committee, its method of operation, and its authority in order to achieve objectives is published in a separate document.

In Elm Grove's promulgation, membership of the Interdisciplinary Committee is composed of the administrator, or his designee; the medical director; the director of Health Services, who, in this case, is also the associate administrator; the director of Social Services; and a representative of the Board of Directors. The Board member, the promulgation states, may be the advocate for the resident-in-review to assure objectivity.

One must question when the promulgation does not include oversight of the Committee's action by the Board of Directors or by governmental statute. One must also question the qualifications, apathy, or empathy of the representative of the Board of Directors who is the designated member of the Committee to be the advocate of the resident-in-review so as to assure objectivity. Objectivity implies an unbiased and detached opinion. Certainly when an advocate reviews the situation he must do so in an impersonal manner with absolutely no preconceived ideas. One really must question the entire membership of the Committee itself, its chairpersons, and the degree of objectivity they all may harbor concerning the resident-in-review in an administration with obedient and perhaps fearing subordinates.

But, according to the promulgation, the representative of the Board, with his objectivity and his designation as advocate for the resident-in-review; the resident-in-review himself; or the resident's surrogate; cannot over-ride the decision of the membership of the Committee. The decision of the Committee is final and binding on the disposition of the case before it with the resident-in-review its sole subject, and implementation of its verdict—that is, deciding the resident's destiny—is delegated to the administrator. The promulgation provides no mechanism for appeal.

Thus, the administrator and his associate, both having direct supervision over all members, except perhaps one, can influence, if not dominate, the decisions of the Committee if they have the will to do so.

The Life Care Agreement, also, provides authority to the administrator, and to his associate, since the associate has deputy capacity, for disciplinary action against a resident, and involuntary eviction. But, this authority allows them to act alone according to their own volition, for there is no provision for a committee's input, or oversight by a higher authority. And, there is no mechanism for appeal indicated, nor insistence for an advocate, or surrogate, to act in the resident's behalf.

The resident is always at the mercy of the administrator—his fairness, kindness, forbearance, and compassion—for the administrator is the resident's custodian of his health, care, and wellbeing. It is the administrator to whom the resident unconditionally grants his health care destiny for the remainder of his life when he enters the Community. Having fallen in disfavor with Elm Grove's administration—its administrator and his associate—and without benefit of family or surrogates, or without benefit of appeal if there were family or surrogates, Carl and I would be seated in Elm Grove directly under a "sword of Damocles".

CHAPTER VIII

"SEVERANCE"

It was early in December 1990 when Carl called Secord, Dike, and Jonz, Attorneys at Law, to ask if Mr. Secord were of a particular religious persuasion and if he had an attorney on his staff with court room experience. We had been residents of Elm Grove for just a year.

We met with Mr. Lloyd Secord and his partner, Mr. Anderson Jonz, to discuss our intentions to leave Elm Grove and their representing us in the severance. Both listened intently. They understood immediately that our complaint involved not money, but principle. Carl and I hoped that Elm Grove's administration and Board would also grasp our resolve. Neither did.

On January 21, 1991 Mr. Secord, Mr. Jonz, Carl and I, and Mr. Near, Ms. Sharpe, and their legal representative met in Elm Grove's conference room. There, our attorneys presented Carl's and my intention to leave.

At this session, in brief, Mr. Jonz stated that although Carl and I had enjoyed some privileges, Elm Grove had misrepresented itself. And, had I been given a respectful audition of my grievances on September 19, there would have been no need for this meeting. Consequently, Carl and I were leaving Elm Grove and we felt we were entitled to a refund of the entrance fee plus the monies spent for improvements to our apartment—improvements we had had no time to enjoy.

Mr. Near rejected the idea that Elm Grove had misrepresented itself. Rather, according to him, our "unhappiness" and our "inability to adjust to life at Elm Grove" lay in the fact that we "expected too much"—more than Elm Grove was capable of providing. He adamantly declared, "And there will be no dickering over money!" He was absolutely correct. Strange as it may seem in a crass world, this suit was about principle, not money.

Following the meeting of January 21, our attorney hand delivered the following letter to Mr. Near, which read in part:

> "On behalf of our clients, kindly consider this to constitute notice of their intention to permanently depart and vacate the above premises at Elm Grove, and to otherwise terminate their relationship with Elm Grove, effective midnight, February 28, 1991.
>
> Nothing herein shall be construed as a waiver of any claims and/or causes of action contemplated by our clients as I related to you in our meeting of January 21, 1991."

Our formal notice of intent to leave was promptly followed by a letter signed by Mr. Near, forwarded to Mr. Jonz through Elm Grove's attorney, setting forth Elm Grove's position in regard to Carl and me. This correspondence read in part:

> "In re: the Lindstrom matter, I would like to convey to Mrs. Lindstrom's lawyers the following thoughts.
>
> There was no misrepresentation. . . . This is a case of the Lindstroms not adjusting to life in this retirement community.
>
> As to the renovations, our contract clearly states that a resident of Elm Grove has no interest in the real estate or improvements and that the Life Care Agreement is for services which carries with it a right of occupancy. . . . The Lindstroms understood this at the time we approved the renovations.
>
> As to the kitchen improvements, they are in reality a nuisance to Elm Grove. . . . I see the kitchen as having no tangible

value to Elm Grove; therefore should the Lindstroms so desire, the committee has authorized me to offer the Lindstroms the option to take the kitchen equipment and cabinets with them when they leave. If the Lindstroms want the kitchen we would need to inspect the improvements to verify to the mutual agreement of the parties the items which the Lindstroms would be entitled to remove.

It is clear that the Lindstroms are not happy here. It is not our desire to have them stay here and continue to engage in confrontational behavior which is disruptive to the smooth operation of the facility. Since both parties would like the Lindstroms to find other living accommodations there is no reason why we should not be able to settle this matter."

/s/ Robert Near
Executive Director

Ironic, that during Carl's and my entire period of residency, until now, we had not been told by Mr. Near that we were "confrontational" and "disruptive," and if we did not "adjust" we were not wanted. Instead, we were readily granted permission to renovate our kitchen to the tune of many thousands of dollars, and make other upgrades to the tune of thousands more.

Obviously Near and Sharpe must have seethed and held grudges when Carl and I dared to express our grievances and criticisms concerning services they provided—or did not provide—services that we, including the helpless patients in Ashley House whom I assisted, had every right to receive, and with the excellence we had every right to expect.

If Near's letter had not maligned Carl's and my character, we could have laughed at Near's suggestion that, like a couple of turtles, we carry our beautiful kitchen—appliances, cabinets, and all—across the country on our backs while we searched for a new Life Care Community to call home. But where, pray tell, would we find a Community which would accept us with Near's accusation that we "couldn't adjust" and by engaging in "confrontational behavior" we "disrupted Elm Grove"? Who would want us?

So Carl and I raised our demands for settlement. To the terms, in addition to the return of our entire entrance fee and monies spent in upgrading our apartment, we now would require an apology from Mr. Near for maligning us; and from both Near and Sharpe, an apology for their disrespect when they harassed me in September. But with this we hit a stalemate.

The plans to vacate Elm Grove moved ahead. We located a rental and moved out before February 28. Since Tuesday had been our scheduled cleaning day, our monthly maintenance fee had been paid for the month of February. Before we turned in the key I wanted someone to inspect and pass judgment on this unit which we had vacated. So on February 26 we awoke to one final trip to Elm Grove.

The housekeeper should have arrived at 12:45 P.M. but no one appeared. I stood in the doorway of the empty apartment waiting for the person assigned to do the cleaning when three housekeepers sauntered down the hall. I asked which one was to clean my apartment. No one knew. They looked in the empty unit and the eldest of the three asked, "Is your husband the military officer who's so very important?" To me he is important, so with a straight face, I said, "Oh, yes!" But certainly Mr. Near had been correct when he told me the staff was privy to all information about the residents.

"Has he been transferred?"

I merely said that he was retired.

It wasn't until 1:15 P.M. that I finally reached the housekeeping supervisor who personally came to the apartment to clean my bathrooms and run the sweeper. She assured me that I didn't have to clean for the apartments are always cleaned when someone moves in. Remembering how the admissions director couldn't explain how our apartment had fallen through the cracks and remembering, too, that this was the same woman who didn't think I wanted their old drapes just a year ago, I merely refrained from commenting.

When she finished in less than 15 minutes I asked if she would verify the fact that we had left our apartment at Elm Grove in a satisfactory condition. Her answer, "No one had ever left an apartment looking like this one!"

We turned in our key and left.

Throughout this whole ordeal we had been determined that we would not upset any of the elderly residents with our reason for leaving. We merely offered the comment that Mr. Secord had suggested when we were asked the reason for our move: "Elm Grove is not for us." But through the grapevine I learned that we were going because although Mrs. Lindstrom liked it here her husband was unhappy. Unhappy? Carl was absolutely furious when he sat in Mr. Secord's office for that first time and told our attorney that no one was going to talk to his wife like Near and Sharpe had done and get away with it!

The rumor that had us leaving because I was going off to join the troops in the Persian Gulf (this was during the Persian Gulf War) really amused both of us. That could only have originated at the beauty shop when someone's hearing aid had been turned down while I was expounding about the activists who were demonstrating against the war and I said if I were younger I'd volunteer.

March passed quickly with our settling in at the new residence and with consultations with Mr. Jonz over the preparations of our complaint against Elm Grove. Finally it was ready.

CHAPTER IX

"THE NEWS ARTICLE"

Anderson Jonz prepared our complaint with us, the Lindstroms, as plaintiffs, Elm Grove, Inc., as the defendant. The complaint, to be filed in the County Court of Common Pleas, was entitled, "Notice to Defend and Claim Rights". The case was not taken on a contingency basis.

Elm Grove's attorney was aware that a complaint was being prepared and he asked Mr. Jonz for a copy before it was presented to the court. Thus arose the following correspondence.

March 27, 1991

Jack Fulton Osterhauser, Esquire

RE: Carl A. Lindstrom and Virginia K. Lindstrom v. Elm Grove

Dear Mr. Osterhauser:

Enclosed please find true and correct photocopy of Complaint with respect to the above matter.

As we discussed in our previous telephone conversation, I am forwarding this photocopy to you as a courtesy, so that you may discuss this matter with your client before litigation is formally commenced.

Accordingly, should we not hear from you on or before April 3, 1991, we will be constrained to file the original with the Court of Common Pleas on Thursday, April 4, 1991.

As you may recall, in order to avoid litigation, the following must occur:

1. Remittance by Elm Grove to our clients of their entry fee ($138,000.00) and the funds invested by Mr. and Mrs. Lindstrom in their unit ($13,558.00);

2. A formal written apology must be received from Mr. Near and Ms. Sharpe for their treatment of Mrs. Lindstrom.

Of course, should you wish to discuss this matter further, please do not hesitate to contact me.

Sincerely,
SECORD, DIKE & JONZ
/s/ Lloyd Secord

LS: x
enclosure
cc: Mr. and Mrs. Carl A. Lindstrom

April 3, 1991 came without response from Elm Grove. On April 4, 1991 the complaint was filed, and a diligent court reporter from a local newspaper picked up the complaint at the court house and emblazoned it in bold headlines in their Sunday edition, April 7, 1991—"Couple Sue Retirement Village—Complain about treatment of patients."

The news release shook the community, and Elm Grove's residents seemingly and understandably were upset, for the adminstrator distributed the following letter, and, as I was informed, was busy taking testimonials. Since the co-signer of Mr. Near's letter to the residents was the chairman of the Board of Directors, it was obvious that the Board approved and supported Mr. Near and would stand by him in court.

April 9, 1991

Dear Resident,

As you undoubtedly know by now, Elm Grove has been named in a suit by former residents of the community. Sunday's local paper contained an article which quoted several portions of the suit.

We have met with our attorneys and have instructed them to defend Elm Grove in a vigorous manner. We are not at liberty to say too much at this time, but wish to inform you that we consider these charges baseless and that we have every expectation that we will be successful in our defense of the litigation.

We appreciate all of your messages of support over the past several days and will endeavor to keep you informed of our progress within the limitations of the litigation process.

Sincerely,

Chairman of the Board   Executive Director

As noted in Near's letter to the residents, he had thanked them for their messages of support—for the multitude of letters, which I was told, poured into his office. One of the saccharine letters was even published in Elm Grove's OUTLOOK, a sleek quarterly publication distributed to prospective residents on the waiting list. Its intent was obvious.

Testimonials written by residents who had been convalescent patients in Ashley House after a hospital stay, could, without a doubt, extol treatment there as exemplary—such patients could fend for themselves. The convalescing resident, however, was not my concern—the helpless, incapacitated, or incompetent patients in Ashley House were. Only one other resident of Elm Grove, in addition to myself, had volunteered her services to help feed incompetent or incapacitated patients in Ashley's dining room at the evening meal while I was there. None of the residents, during my sojourn as a volunteer, almost nightly for eight months, ever visited to observe the gerichair patients lined up against the wall being fed unappetizing goo of mixed pureed foods, spooned into hesitant mouths. None watched milk and juice fed with indifference and insensitivity by the aides to wash down the foods patients had pouched in their cheeks, or which they were unable to chew sufficiently to swallow. None volunteered to assist those helpless individuals when I appealed to the Residents Association—an appeal to talk with patients and feed them in a respectful manner so that they might feel someone cared—that they hadn't been abandoned.

How many times did I hear Elm Grove residents say, "If ever I am a patient in Ashley House, I hope I have enough money to hire a private aide." I could be wrong. Perhaps the residents really were aware of the woes awaiting them at meal times if they became incapacitated or incompetent patients in Ashley House. Perhaps they knew that Elm Grove's "good enough" philosophy abounded everywhere—even in the Ashley dining room. But with Elm Grove's denial of advocacy on behalf of the patients, other than by staff, their private aides will have no rights to bring anything to the attention of the administrator, or staff, for the aide would be told, "Feed everything on the tray and be quiet. Don't question, don't express opinions, don't make observations nor recommendations and don't complain. Just feed."

There comes to mind a sympathetic and caring private aide who picked one of the thousands of daffodils growing in profusion in Elm Grove's gardens to brighten her patient's tray, and at her patient's request. She was reported to the administrator, summoned to his office, admonished, and told not to do that again or she would not be allowed to return to Elm Grove. So much for private aides.

"Good enough" may be Elm Grove's standard, but, to me, Elm Grove's "good enough" is not good enough for "The Cadillac" of retirement communities. There should be excellence in both food provided and treatment of all Ashley patients at dinner time in a polite, kind, and dignified manner. There should be excellence in food quality and preparation, and excellence in food service and supervision—all sprinkled liberally with empathy and politeness. Foreboding as the thought may be—all of the authors of those "love letters" which came pouring into Near's office may one day find Ashley House their final abode.

CHAPTER X

"THE COMPLAINT"

Carl's and my complaint read, in part:

Shortly after joining defendant's community, plaintiff undertook to volunteer her time, services, and energy at defendant's skilled nursing facility.

At the facility plaintiff volunteered to feed and assist in the care of elderly residents of defendant's community, who were no longer able to care for themselves.

During the period of time plaintiff was assigned to assist two female residents with their feeding and, during the course of that period developed a friendship with them, as well as an opportunity to observe their reaction to certain foods which were prepared by defendant for their evening meal.

More specifically, but without limitation, plaintiff noticed that one of the patients to whom she was assigned would frequently evidence gastric reactions to a number of the foods which plaintiff was required to feed her, and on occasion choked on some of the heavier bits of food on her tray, on further occasion, but without limitation, plaintiff noted that both her patients would be unable to swallow certain foods, without chewing for inordinately long periods of time.

As she made the aforesaid observations, plaintiff would report same to members of defendant's nursing staff, who in turn represented to plaintiff that they would act upon her observations and direct defendant's kitchen to modify those patients' trays of food in order to accommodate their particular needs, i.e., by pureeing food and/or providing for foods which were easier to chew, swallow, and digest.

However, despite the aforesaid representations, over the span of approximately six months, defendant persisted in providing food which was difficult for the patients to eat and/or digest.

Accordingly, plaintiff presented her concerns to defendant's Clinical Dietitian, in an effort to present her concerns to a level within defendant's administration which could take appropriate action.

In order to organize her thoughts with her meeting with defendant's Clinical Dietitian, plaintiff prepared a collection of written notes summarizing her observations and concerns over the past six months, and read same to the dietitian.

Included within plaintiff notes, all of which were read to the Clinical Dietitian, was a statement that she was prepared to take her complaints and observations to state and federal governmental officials if defendant did not take steps to correct the problem.

Defendant's Clinical Dietitian insisted that plaintiff turn over to her those notes, presumably to provide the Dietitian an opportunity to analyze plaintiff's complaints and observations.

However, approximately six days after her meeting with defendant's Clinical Dietitian, plaintiff was summoned to a meeting with defendant's Executive Director, and his Associate.

The meeting was conducted in defendant's Executive Director's office and plaintiff was not afforded an opportunity to have accompany her either her husband or another advocate.

During the course of that meeting plaintiff was subjected to abusive tone and language by both the Executive Director and Associate Director who often talked to her in raised voices, with demanding and condescending tones.

At that meeting, plaintiff was admonished for rendering criticisms and/or opinion of her observations regarding the quality, kind and form of food defendant was providing to its patients.

Plaintiff was further admonished that she had no right to express any observations regarding the response of any of the patients nor had any right whatsoever to express criticisms of any kind regarding their treatment and/or care.

Furthermore, plaintiff was threatened with a libel suit for making the statements contained in her notes and/or if she referred her complaints to government officials, and was further threatened that state agencies could bring charges against her for not feeding all the food on the patients' trays.

Additionally, plaintiff was told by defendant's Executive Director and his Associate that she could continue to be a volunteer so long as she expressed no opinions or criticisms of what she observed of patient care at the facility.

The meeting was terminated after one and $1/4$ hours by defendant's Executive Director, who thereupon warned plaintiff in the following manner, 'I do not intend to have this meeting again.'

Notwithstanding the foregoing plaintiff made additional observations and/or criticisms to defendant's Clinical Dietitian, in a written memorandum.

Approximately one week thereafter, plaintiff was no longer allowed to feed patients for whom she had been caring for approximately seven months, and was only allowed to feed patients in a small room, isolated from the rest of the facility.

Exhibits for the complaint included my notes which I had read to the Elm Grove dietitian (shown in Chapter III), my letter to the Elm Grove dietitian complaining of the treatment of Tricia after her encounter with the dentist (shown in Chapter VI), "Resident/ Patient Rights" published and distributed by the Elm Grove Board of Directors, and "Patient Rights" in *Long Term Care Facilities Licensure Regulations*, Pennsylvania Department of Health.

Elm Grove, in its objections called the complaint "shotgun" and advised the court that it need not submit itself to "eyestrain" in granting Elm Grove a favorable decision.

In its objections to the complaint, Elm Grove chose not to defend itself against the charges. Instead it opted for demurrer which is a plea for dismissal of a lawsuit by a defendant on the grounds that even if the facts as stated in the complaint were admitted by the defendant as true, they were insufficient as set forth to constitute a cause for action.

The court granted Elm Grove's plea for demurrer and Carl's and my complaint was refused a hearing in public court. Thus Elm Grove was not required under law to admit to, or deny, the charges.

Carl and I had claimed rights published in Elm Grove's "Resident/Patient Rights" which were established by its Board of Directors as an "expression of its deep concern for each person as an individual of dignity and worth". These rights included among others, the right:

— to receive proper care and attention from physician and staff;
— to be involved in the planning of one's total care;
— to establish advanced directives through a Living Will;
— to be free from mental and physical abuse;
— to exercise rights as a citizen;
— to communicate grievances, complaints, or recommendations without fear of reprisal, or deprivation of any kind; and to reasonable attention to these grievances and complaints;
— to considerate and respectful care at all times; and
— to the preservation of individual dignity.

However, despite the Board of Directors' concern for "each person" as an individual of dignity and worth, Elm Grove argued that its "Resident/Patient Rights" were solely in place for those residents confined as patients in its long-term care facility, and could not be claimed by any independent-resident.

The court accepted this argument and Carl and I, as independent-residents, were consequently denied all the rights listed in Elm Grove's "Resident/Patient Rights". So, too, thereby, all independent-residents in Elm Grove had these rights willfully and legally abolished by the administration and supported by court order.

Carl and I, as independent-residents, had appealed to the court to imply to us, as well as to all Elm Grove independent-residents, those rights granted in Pennsylvania's *Long Term Care Facilities Licensure Regulations* for patients in Elm Grove's care facility. Accepting Elm Grove's argument that Carl and I were not patients but at all times were independent-residents, the court denied us the rights as expressed in that document—rights which the Board of Directors had mirrored in Elm Grove's "Resident/Patient Rights".

To further seal its objections, Elm Grove argued that none of the rights in its Board of Directors', "Resident/Patient Rights," were contractually relevant for Carl and me as independent-residents since they were not explicit in the contractual agreement which we had signed. The court agreed.

Thus Carl and I, by court decree, were refused a legal right, as independent-residents in Elm Grove, to communicate grievances, complaints, or recommendations to the Elm Grove staff or to outside representatives of choice without fear of reprisal, discrimination, or deprivation of any kind; to reasonable attention by Elm Grove to those grievances; to exercise rights as citizens; and to be treated with consideration, respect and full recognition of dignity and individuality. All of these rights would have been sufficient to support our cause and allow our complaint to be heard in public court.

But not only did Elm Grove abolish the rights of its independent-residents but the rights of its patients were also trampled.

Elm Grove argued in its plea for dismissal of Carl's and my complaint that I, as an independent-resident and volunteer, had no rights (a) to bring complaints of abuse or mistreatment of my charges to administrative, medical, or nursing staff; or to governmental regulatory agencies, (b) to report observations of my charges' adverse responses and signs of illness, or (c) to express opinions, recommendations, and suggestions for the betterment of my charges, unless I were my patient's guardian, my patient was a co-complaint, and I had professional expertise to support the complaint. Further, Elm Grove argued that it was not responsible for the program of feeding helpless patients in its long-term care facility, Ashley House: rather the volunteer feeding of patients, therein, is arranged for and sponsored by the Community's Residents Association, a non-administrative body of residents separate and distinct from the administration. (See chart on the following page.)

Although such arguments are contrary to provisions of health care statutes of the Commonwealth of Pennsylvania and of the federal government, the court sustained Elm Grove's position. Thus, Carl's and my claim of rights of patients in Elm Grove's long-term care facility to unrestricted advocacy on their behalf when their abuse is observed, and unrestricted rights of volunteers—indeed, of anyone—who attempt to assist them to exercise their rights and to advocate for them were obliterated by court order. These rights, too, would have been sufficient to support Carl's and my cause and allow the complaint to be heard in public court.

When I complained to Mr. Near and Ms. Sharpe about the quality and form of food being fed to the incompetent and incapacitated elderly patients in Ashley House and advocated for their betterment, Elm Grove, in its argument to support its objections to Carl's and my complaint, claimed that such actions constituted interference with prescribed diets, second-guessing the prescription of the Elm Grove physician and dietitian; claiming legal rights to perform volunteer services; and claiming proprietary rights to feed such patients and advocate on their behalf. The court again agreed.

But all of the foregoing aside, Elm Grove's most tenacious argument for dismissal of Carl's and my complaint as presented by their attorney was based predominantly and repeatedly on:

". . . all of the material facts of the Complaint and all of plaintiff wife's claims arise solely from her pleaded subjective and idio-

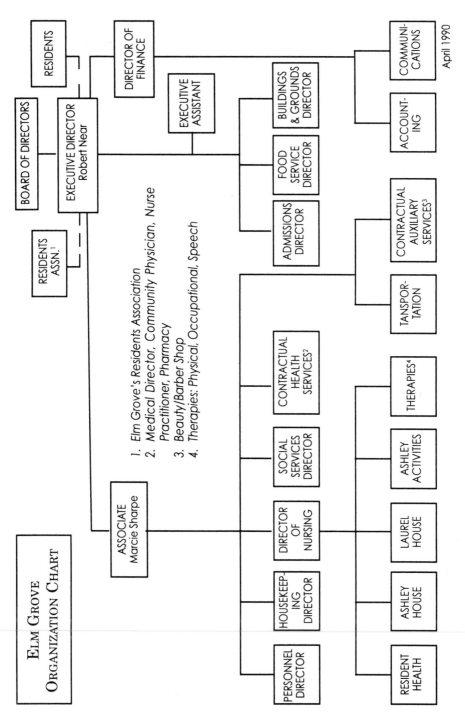

ELM GROVE
ORGANIZATION CHART

April 1990

BOARD OF DIRECTORS

RESIDENTS

RESIDENTS ASSN.[1]

EXECUTIVE DIRECTOR
Robert Near

DIRECTOR OF FINANCE

EXECUTIVE ASSISTANT

ASSOCIATE
Marcie Sharpe

1. Elm Grove's Residents Association
2. Medical Director, Community Physician, Nurse Practitioner, Pharmacy
3. Beauty/Barber Shop
4. Therapies: Physical, Occupational, Speech

BUILDINGS & GROUNDS DIRECTOR

FOOD SERVICE DIRECTOR

ADMISSIONS DIRECTOR

COMMUNI-CATIONS

ACCOUNT-ING

CONTRACTUAL AUXILIARY SERVICES[3]

TRANSPOR-TATION

CONTRACTUAL HEALTH SERVICES[2]

SOCIAL SERVICES DIRECTOR

DIRECTOR OF NURSING

HOUSEKEEP-ING DIRECTOR

PERSONNEL DIRECTOR

THERAPIES[4]

ASHLEY ACTIVITIES

LAUREL HOUSE

ASHLEY HOUSE

RESIDENT HEALTH

syncratic opinions on the feeding of certain elderly patients (others) none of which (*sic*) are plaintiffs herein or represented by plaintiffs as any sort of guardian, and represent second-guessing the prescriptions of a Community Physician and the work of the Clinical Dietitian."

". . . the Complaint *focuses* upon a childhood grievance when Mrs. Lindstrom's ulcer was misdiagnosed . . . and she has nursed the ulcer all her life, so that the thought of acidic food upsets her."

"We respectfully represent that your Honorable Court need not be subjected to additional eyestrain to grant Demurrer . . . based upon the *perceived* violations of the rights of others not party to the proceeding."

". . . *all* of the material facts of the Complaint and all of plaintiff wife's claims arise solely from her pleaded *subjective* and *idiosyncratic* opinions on the feeding of certain elderly persons."

When Elm Grove's attorney accused me of idiosyncratic and subjective opinions it was without benefit of a psychological or psychiatric evaluation. He accused me of opinions that the normal person doesn't harbor—opinions that denote a mental derangement. According to this attorney I harbored opinions that existed only in my mind and, therefore, such imaginings could not be checked or verified by anyone. As I studied his writings I wondered if this were an insidious and devious attempt to portray this 72-year-old as an addled and less than competent person? Did he think for one moment that I had imagined the nightly trays that brought on violent coughing spells? Had I just imagined that Merrie, the charge nurse, had used as her excuse for putting me out of the Ashley dining room that she had heard Tricia coughing so violently "the other night when I was alone with her in the dining room" that she was going to reassign me to feed Hope and relegate Tricia to the care of the aides before something tragic happened? I wanted to know who at this institution was checking on the trays prescribed by the doctor and dietitian when they came into Ashley's dining room at night. Certainly the dietitian, under the doctor's direction, could order clear jello for the 'Tricias' and 'Johns' but since the kitchen's menus were prepared for the 'mainstream' as Mr. Near had espoused, they might be laced with nuts or celery. Who supervised the young aides who placed the 'mainstream' jello on the trays when the doctor and dietitian had called for jello without nuts and celery? Did such a question not reflect reality? On three consecutive nights just before Hope died I complained that her broth marked "strained" on her menu, and ordered as such by the doctor and dietitian, was delivered filled with meat, rice, and vegetables. I had intelligence enough, or was it, as Elm Grove's attorney pleaded, abnormal behavior, to read the menu before feeding Hope and I spooned out just the liquid; but what unsupervised aide who fed such patients would bother to do this? What unsupervised aide filled that mug with solid foods in the first place? These were my objections. The Community's physician and dietitian may be prescribing dietary services for the patients but the patients were not receiving them. And it was, and is, my contention that I had a right, under the law, to object to such treatment—even at the expense of being considered of peculiar temperament. Moreover, I had a moral right to object to patient abuse—mine or otherwise—without such objections being deemed subjective and idiosyncratic.

But again the court sustained Elm Grove's arguments, presented as such, in their entirety.

I must make note of one more statement of Elm Grove's attorney in his plea for demurrer. He wrote in his argument for dismissal of the complaint that I was "contacted to <u>discuss</u> my notes to the dietitian."

I find it necessary to underline the word, "discuss,"—a word which denotes civility. Instead, I was summoned by a phone call during which Mr. Near's secretary said bluntly, "Mr. Near wants to see you in his office tomorrow at 3:30 P.M.!" I wasn't politely contacted with, "Can you be there?" or, "Is it convenient, since I understand you have a guest? Would you be able to stop by tomorrow at 3:30 P.M. so we can discuss your notes to Belle?" No indeed! There was no civility in that blunt summons, "Mr. Near wants to see you in his office tomorrow at 3:30 P.M.!" No mention was made of the fact that Ms. Sharpe would be there too, else I would have said, "I certainly will bring my husband with me." My Arizona house guest was just getting ready to leave for the airport when I turned from the phone to relay Near's message to Carl and Betty. "Wow!" exclaimed Betty, "You're being called to the principal's office. What did you do?"

It is inconceivable to me, that Mr. Near, Ms. Sharpe, and their attorney had judged that Carl and I had no rights under the Life Care Agreement, under law, under the Constitution, or under the policies of the Board of Directors while we had lived, as residents, in Elm Grove. It had been stressed, upon entering Elm Grove, that we were not being institutionalized. But, it is obvious, now, that we had been. In retrospect, it was with this belief that Near and Sharpe had admonished me and mandated that I would not question, I might not complain, I should not dissent—rather that I must conform, I should accept, and I would be obedient.

If ours had been a "shot gun" complaint as Jack F. Osterhauser had dubbed it, one can only wonder what adjective could be used to describe his defense. Anderson Jonz had reminded the court that "for the purpose of testing the legal sufficiency of a complaint, a DEMURRER admits as true all well-pleaded material and relevant facts. If the facts, as pleaded, state a cause for which relief may be granted under any theory of law a DEMURRER must be denied."

Unfortunate for us—and for all independent-residents and patients in Elm Grove—Judge Warren Mark did not agree.

CHAPTER XI

"THE JUDGE"

The statues and paintings of Justice always depict this blind goddess holding a scale in one hand and a two-edged sword in the other. As a child I was told that she was the symbol of impartiality and fairness—dispensing justice to all who encountered her—hence, the blindfold. With age and cynicism I doubted that explanation. I began to believe she wore the blindfold because she couldn't stand what she saw and with Judge Warren Mark's decision of August 27, 1991 there was no doubt about it.

Despite the writings of Elm Grove's attorney, despite the thoughtfully researched and beautifully presented "Memorandum of Law in Opposition to Defendant's Preliminary Objections" by Anderson Jonz, on the 27th day of August 1991, Judge Mark of the Court of Common Pleas handed down his decision—not by signing his name but merely initialing the form presented to him by J. F. Osterhauser, Elm Grove's attorney. No oral or written opinion of his own accompanied his initials—merely the date.

It was apparent, by Judge Mark's ruling, that he wholeheartedly supported Elm Grove's pleadings and arguments in their entirety. Would the dozen or so residents of Elm Grove—all former attorneys and one a former Pennsylvania judge—agree with Judge Mark and Elm Grove's legal staff in denying Carl and me access to a court of law to defend our rights as citizens and rights provided by state and federal health care statutes? Could they morally and ethically condone Elm Grove's administrator and his associate who act as a law unto themselves and thereby are able to declare, under authority of their position, that they can at will abrogate all my rights and those of others in their Community?

The Judge had rendered his verdict, and on September 12, 1991 at 8:50 A.M. from the Office of the Prothonotary, came the summary of the case of Carl A. and Virginia K. Lindstrom vs Elm Grove. Conspicuously typed at the bottom of the page were these words in capital letters—END OF CASE. But Judge Mark and Elm Grove were premature if they believed that. Robert Near and Marcie Sharpe must not be allowed to harass, threaten, and intimidate any more elderly residents. They would be held accountable for their actions if we had to take our case all the way to the Supreme Court. What babes in the woods we were when we told Anderson Jonz to appeal.

CHAPTER XII

"THE APPEAL"

On September 19, 1991 Anderson Jonz informed Judge Mark and Jack F. Osterhauser that Carl and I were filing a Notice of Appeal, and since Judge Mark had sustained Elm Grove's objections striking and dismissing our complaint with no written opinion of his own, there was no transcript to be ordered.

The appeal was presented in a logical and succinct form. Mr. Jonz concluded by stating that Carl and I did plead our case properly with specific cause of action for each count and he charged that the lower court had erred in sustaining Elm Grove's objections. He requested that the order of the lower court of August 27, 1991 be reversed, stating that, "The matter should therefore be remanded with instructions that Elm Grove's objections be overruled, and Elm Grove be directed to answer the complaint."

Judge Mark answered, "We disagree". "No contest was pled", "There was no eviction, constructive or otherwise", "Lindstroms' averments completely lack specificity"—one page of double-spaced notes, little more than the initials and date that Elm Grove had asked this judge to fill in on August 27, 1991.

Elm Grove's counter statement of the case submitted to the Court of Appeals, Philadelphia, Pennsylvania in February 1992 began with this doggerel:

> "Jack Sprat could eat no fat,
> His wife could eat no lean —
> Whatever else you make of that
> They did quite well between"
> Mother Goose

I retrieved a copy of this brief from my mailbox on Valentine's Day, 1992. Years ago, in a children's literature course as an undergraduate at the University of Pittsburgh, I learned that Mother Goose rhymes, even altered ones, were not meant to amuse children. They were written as political satire to poke fun at someone or something. Jack F. Osterhauser, Esq. had successfully guided his client through the lower court by dubbing me idiosyncratic, by suggesting that I imagined run-ins with Elm Grove's staff and administration, by insinuating that I wasn't quite with it. Could we really expect anything different this time around with such an introduction?

To answer that question, this counter statement to our case ran true to form. Mr. Osterhauser had been successful once. Why change his modus operandi? The Court was told that:

"The contract (our agreement with Elm Grove) to be avoided (was) on dietary issues involving others."

". . .Mrs. Lindstrom has had perceived run-ins with Elm Grove personnel." (underlining added)

"As pleaded all of the material facts relate to plaintiff's subjective and idiosyncratic opinions of her perceived abuse of others." (underlining added)

The counter statement also included again the accounting of the Elm Grove Residents Association's separate-and-distinct role in volunteer feeding of patients, of the administration's kindly effort to "discuss" my observations when I had been summoned to their office, my belief that I had some sort of right to perform voluntary services—all of which had been presented to the lower court. There was, however, one new statement which certainly could bolster the idea that I harbored idiosyncratic ideas, perceived and subjective opinions. This quote reads as follows:

> "Elm Grove's mission includes by way of example, dealing with insanity and dangerous diseases short of hospitalization."

Was there a reason for including this statement?

Mr. Osterhauser asserted that after my meeting with Mr. Near and Miss Sharpe Carl and I had concluded that our agreement with Elm Grove "would be breached in the future". The fact that I had learned at the meeting of September 19 that I had no rights to complain of abuse or mistreatment of the helpless patients in Ashley House, nor to advocate for their betterment, meant no one would be permitted to advocate for me if ever I found myself in their position. Additionally, I was told that my advanced dietary directive for my Living Will was useless; I was forbidden to consult with the medical director in the planning of my care; and I learned that my dietary needs and concerns would not be addressed nor accommodated if I were unable to fit into Elm Grove's 'mainstream' feeding program. All of this eliminated a "future" decision to leave Elm Grove. My "future" was breached at that meeting.

CHAPTER XIII

"THE HEARING"

Prior to the disposition of our case by the three judges of the Court of Appeals it was necessary to have the attorney for the Lindstroms and the attorney for Elm Grove appear before the court in person to provide oral arguments in addition to their written briefs. The date was set for April 21, 1992 at 9:30 A.M. in Room 2001 of the Old Federal Building, corner of 5th and Market Streets in Philadelphia. We had never observed Anderson Jonz in action. We knew Osterhauser only through his writings, so we looked forward to attending this hearing.

Surely a taxi would be our best means of transportation at this early hour since we were unfamiliar with Philadelphia's one-way streets and other traffic patterns. What a wise decision, for with a pea-soup fog, early morning business traffic, a pile-up on Interstate 95, and misinformation about the location of the hearing we arrived at the courtroom just five minutes before the Court of Appeals convened.

The room was crowded with attorneys representing appellants and appellees. If there were any other spectators they weren't discernible. Certainly no one from Elm Grove was there.

The presiding judge laid the ground rules—present your argument in 20 minutes—allow yourself three minutes for rebuttal if need be and cases droned on.

Just before the morning break after which our case was to be presented by Mr. Jonz first, answered by Osterhauser, Carl and I moved to a side chair to sit directly in line with both attorneys and within ear shot of the three judges. When our case was called all resentment we had felt at being directed to the wrong building was dispelled. Anderson Jonz more than met our expectations. In a loud, firm voice he greeted the three judges and began his argument by saying, "I want to tell you what this case is not about—it is not about food nor the feeding thereof. Nor is it about proprietary rights! Rather it is about the rights granted by PA Code 28, the "Resident/Patient Rights" granted by Elm Grove's Board of Directors, and the rights granted under federal legislation—all of which have been denied to Mrs. Lindstrom who has been described by the appellee as "idiosyncratic" with "perceived notions" of what she was allowed to do. He laid out a firm case for the residents in the independent section of the Continuing Care Retirement Community stating that such Communities were hybrids—hence, they have no direct legislation. But in reality everyone in the independent section of a Continuing Care Retirement Community is a patient by virtue of their treatment by the medical director from the time of entrance. He ended his presentation by pointing out that the Lindstroms had paid $138,000 for their apartment—up front money which had to be paid before moving in; that they had spent an additional $12,000 refurbishing their apartment which was to be their home for the rest of their days in the independent section of Elm Grove; and on top of that $150,000 they had paid approximately $30,000 in monthly maintenance fees. Mrs. Lindstrom was 72 years old; and a mature, intelligent woman of that age did not expect for her $180,000 to be treated like a wayward child—scolded, harassed, threatened with a law suit by the administrator of the facility who had *summoned* her to his office and told her, as a final warning, that he did not intend to have this meeting again. Anderson Jonz had brought tears to my eyes for he had zeroed in on all my complaints.

And then it was Jack Fulton Osterhauser's turn. He had sat through Mr. Jonz's presentation in a sideways position with his head bowed as though he were examining his shoes, never looking at Anderson Jonz nor at the judges. Now he arose stepped to the lectern and began to mumble something to the effect that the Lindstroms had moved to Elm Grove and shortly after, through the Elm Grove Residents Association, had begun to feed two old patients in Ashley House. He continued, "She began to complain although Mr. Lindstrom had made no complaints."

I was straining desperately to follow his mumbled allegations as were the judges for one spoke sharply saying, "Speak up so we can hear you!"

He mumbled something more which I could only assume must have been an apology and then, in a voice more audible, he said that Mrs. Lindstrom prepared a letter to the dietitian in which Mrs. Lindstrom said that she had aversions to certain foods and, therefore, she maintained that her patients should not be fed these foods. She had no right to make such statements not merely because she didn't like those foods but because she was not a patient in Ashley House—she was only a resident at Elm Grove.

Then he informed the court that the Lindstroms were at Elm Grove more than three months so Elm Grove gave them the contractual severance payment of $77,000. That was all they were entitled to.

He didn't address any of the counts in the case as laid out by Mr. Jonz and in approximately three minutes he said that he, like Judge Warren Mark last August, would be brief. And he sat down. Whereupon one of the judges said quite sarcastically, "Brief indeed!"

Anderson Jonz asked for rebuttal time which the presiding judge refused. I'm sorry I hadn't timed Mr. Jonz's oral argument to determine if he had some time remaining, and had I known that no record is made of this oral hearing I certainly would have made note.

The contrast of presentations between Anderson Jonz and Elm Grove's attorney could be likened to a debate between Clarence Darrow and a sophomore on a high school debating team, and Anderson Jonz was not the high school sophomore. By his demeanor Osterhauser seemed most ill at ease. Having had nothing previously to judge him by except his writings we tried to determine the reason for his bizarre behavior. We were of the opinion that Mr. Jonz had completely overwhelmed him with his argument and splendid delivery. But were there other contributing reasons for his obvious desire to distance himself from this place and this situation as soon as possible? Had our presence in that court room—sitting so close, leaning forward so eagerly to hear what he said—ruffled him? Surely not! Had he mumbled to keep other attorneys present from hearing that the prestigious Elm Grove was being sued? I think not for each attorney seemed engrossed in his own affairs. Or, in a charitable mood—had he, too, had a rough trip into Philadelphia in the fog? Time will tell—for we, with growing impatience, waited for the decision of the three judges of the Court of Appeals. We hoped that it was taking so long because this was absolutely a "weighty" and not merely a "wait-y" matter. The weeks rolled by—long interminable weeks—six, eight, ten, twelve, fourteen, and finally, after 16 weeks the decision was handed down.

CHAPTER XIV

"CHARACTER ASSASSINATION"

Old "Defender" took his ax
And gave the plaintiff 40 wacks!
And when they saw what he had done
The judges gave her 41!

The decision from the Court of Appeals with the presiding judge offering the judgment read, "We affirm the order sustaining the appellee's DEMURRER in this case." Anderson Jonz had pleaded for dismissal of the lower court's order sustaining demurrer by writing, "Although the law provides no magic formula by which sufficiency of a Complaint can be ascertained, a demurrer should only be sustained in a case free from doubt, and any doubt should be resolved in favor of refusing to enter the demurrer."

Judge Rowe set forth his standard of review as follows:

"Initially we set forth our standard of review. As is our function upon an appeal from a decision of the trial court sustaining preliminary objections in the nature of the demurrer, we must accept as true every relevant fact sufficiently averred in the

<u>plaintiff's complaint together with every inference favorable to the non-moving party which is fairly deducible therefrom.</u>" (Underlining added)

And with this, Judge Rowe in concert with Osterhauser and Judge Mark completed the abolishment of rights of independent residents in Continuing Care Retirement Communities in Pennsylvania—rights granted in Nursing Home Reform Amendments of the Omnibus Budget Reconciliation Act as required by federal statute, rights under Long Term Care Facilities Licensure Regulations of the Pennsylvania Department of Health, rights under Pennsylvania Continuing Care Provider Registration and Disclosure Act, and those listed in Elm Grove's Board of Directors', "Resident/Patient Rights". This was a devastating loss, as Carl and I saw it, to those elderly citizens who had already, or would in the future, put their faith and trust in administrators of Continuing Care Retirement Communities in Pennsylvania—administrators who now have a green light, if such is their will, to govern independent residents in an institutionalized manner with the blessings of the court.

Residents in the independent setting, once the portals of the Community clang shut behind them, were now to all intents and purposes non-entities therein, supported by no statutory or implied rights and will so remain until they become protected under Pennsylvania law as patients in the personal care or long-term care components of the Community. But even then they can claim no rights when grieved unless they themselves are competent enough to demand their rights, or unless, as helpless patients, their advocates are their guardians, have expertise to support complaints, or are their designated co-complainants. So the courts have decreed.

This in itself was a blow. But adding injury to insult Judge Rowe had agreed with Osterhauser's contention that I was idiosyncratic, that I had imagined run-ins with Elm Grove's personnel—in essence, that I belonged to that stereotype of the aging American, Alzheimer-bound, prone to imaginary mischief, not altogether competent. Rowe had been bombarded over and over again by Osterhauser with references to my subjective opinions, to per-

ceived encounters, to my idiosyncratic behavior. Osterhauser
had even included a reference to Elm Grove's mission which, "Included by way of example," said he, "dealing with insanity and
dangerous diseases short of hospitalization." Was all this deliber-
ate repetition meant to have a decisive effect on the reader of
our complaint when he considers "every inference favorable to
the non-moving party which is fairly deducible there from"?

Judge Rowe not only accepted Osterhauser's depiction of
me but he added a further character trait which portrayed me
not only as an idiosyncratic member of the Community but as a
disruptive, confrontational, demanding, and unreasonable shrew
who became so outraged when no one paid attention to me
that I couldn't control myself, so that the kindly Mr. Near and Ms.
Sharpe had no choice but to isolate me in a little room under the
watchful eye of a nurse:

> "Outraged at the inattention of the staff to her concerns, ap-
> pellant wife called upon appellee's clinical dietitian with notes
> of her observations." (Underlining added)

> "The complaint itself, reveals, that despite the considerable dis-
> turbance her complaints caused the appellee's staff, appel-
> lant wife was given a second chance to feed her regular pa-
> tients on the condition that she refrain from further disruptive
> behavior. Because appellant wife found it impossible to so re-
> strain herself, the record indicates the appellee removed ap-
> pellant wife from the care of her original patients but allowed
> her to feed other patients under the close supervision of the
> nursing staff." (Underlining added)

Nowhere in the record, in the complaint, in any of Elm Grove's
objections, or at the hearing before the Court of Appeals in Philadelphia, is there any accusation that I expressed outrage. In-
jected into the record by the court was the fact that I was so
disruptive as a volunteer that I required close supervision by the
nursing staff. I was a bona-fide volunteer for eight months, six
and seven nights a week. If I were so undisciplined or unsatisfactory as the court portrays, I would have been dismissed.

No where in the record is there a charge that I created disturbances among Elm Grove's staff during my volunteerism. The record shows that I was a bona-fide volunteer for six months before the September 19, 1990 meeting with Mr. Near and Ms. Sharpe, and two months following. If I were a disturbance to the staff I would have been dismissed. Contrary to the court's characterization that I was a disturbance, the record shows that the nurses recognized and responded to my observations but were unable to rectify the faults:

> "It's time for pureed foods. I requested this time and time again, but the kitchen doesn't pay attention, but I'll put it down again."

and,

> "Yes, I've asked for more liquids but no one in the kitchen pays attention."

Regarding the court's assertion: ". . . appellant's wife was given a second chance to feed her regular patients on condition that she refrain from further disruptive behavior." The record shows that I was summoned by Near to the meeting of September 19, 1990 (1) solely in response to my request for a meeting with the dietitian when I met with her to ask for an appointment to discuss the patients whom I had fed as a volunteer, (2) to ensure through threats and reprisal, that I refrain from voicing my grievances outside Elm Grove to governmental agencies, and (3) to ensure, by mandate, if I continued as a volunteer, that I cease-and-desist complaints of mistreatment and abuse of the helpless patients whom I fed. No where does the record show that I was accused by Near at the meeting of September 19, 1990, of undisciplined, uncontrolled, unsatisfactory, or disruptive performance or behavior during my prior six months as a volunteer, as the court asserts, and given a second chance by Near and Sharpe to perform obediently. The meeting was called, as the record shows, for only one purpose: for Near and Sharpe to mandate that my future volunteerism be restricted to my total and unconditional silence in the performance of my duties as a feeding volunteer of helpless patients—my advocacy on behalf of helpless patients whom I fed was forbidden and would not be tolerated. If I were as disruptive as the court insists, Near and Sharpe would have dismissed me on the spot.

Regarding the court's assertion: "but allowed to feed other patients under the close supervision of the nursing staff." All volunteers are under the supervision of the nursing staff for such is required under Pennsylvania law. For the court to infer, or conclude, that supervision is not usual but had to be applied solely to me is an untrue portrayal of me as a disruptive and uncontrollable volunteer.

Regarding the court's assertion: "Because appellant's wife found it impossible to restrain herself. . . ." This statement, in concert with Elm Grove's objection to Carl's and my complaint, is a continuation of the Court of Appeals' tenacity in portraying me, throughout its judgment, as a disruptive resident and volunteer of Elm Grove.

Thus, with no substantiation, without providing me due process to counter these accusations, the litigation was dismissed and Carl's and my complaint was refused a hearing in public court. For the Court of Common Pleas and the Court of Appeals to dismiss the complaint and thereby allow their character assassination of me to stand as a matter of public record without affording me due process is a denial of my rights as a citizen of the United States.

Where did Judge Rowe garner the material which prompted his statements, "despite the considerable disturbance her complaint caused the staff", and "that she refrain from further disruptive behavior"? There is nothing in the record, anywhere, in support of, or even to suggest, such judgments. Did it come from Near's correspondence to Elm Grove's attorney and from whom it was forwarded to Mr. Jonz? This letter read, in part:

January 30, 1991
"In re: the Lindstrom matter. I would like to convey to Mrs. Lindstrom's lawyer the following thoughts:

"This is a case of the Lindstroms not adjusting well to life in the retirement community."

"It is not our desire to have them stay here and continue to engage in confrontational behavior which is disruptive to the smooth operation of the facility."

This correspondence never appeared as a matter of record in Elm Grove's objections to Carl's and my complaint or in support of anything. But words contained therein did appear in P. J. Rowe's judgment.

The Court of Appeals, in its judgment, stated:

"It should be noted that nothing appears in the record to suggest that the intended recipients of food complained to appellant wife, nor that she was voicing these concerns at their request."

My charges were helpless, incompetent, and unable to feed themselves let alone speak for themselves. The judge surely was aware of this—it is in the record.

Compounding my unruly and obstreperous behavior as a volunteer as depicted by P. J. Rowe, the court wrote:

"Specifically, appellant wife objected to the fact that the food on the patients' trays was fibrous and needed to be cut in order for the patients to swallow it."

I never objected to fibrous foods as part of my charges' diets when they could ingest such without coughing, choking, or chewing with great difficulty. And I never complained of cutting any foods to accommodate my charges' needs. There is nothing in the record to indicate this.

During our final meeting with Mr. Jonz when he knew how devastated I was by my character assassination which would henceforth stand in court records for all to read, he, who liked to refer to himself as an officer of the court, said, "Well, Judge Rowe could be guilty of judicial error but he had no reason to be so vicious."

That statement prompted Carl and me to file a complaint of ethical misconduct of the judiciary with the Judicial Inquiry and Review Board of the Commonwealth of Pennsylvania. The Board held that when the judiciary, in its orders and judgments for dismissal of complaints of abuse of helpless patients, libels an elderly plaintiff at will by arbitrarily charging the plaintiff—with no substantiation on its part—as idiosyncratic and imagining the abuses set forth in the complaint; arbitrarily and viciously castigates the plaintiff as an uncontrollable ever-complaining shrew with no support for its accusation; introduces fictional scenarios of its own, and misrepresents the complaint; such is but legal error and not contrary to the standards of judicial ethics and conduct, not libelous to the plaintiff in records of the court open to the public, and not in violation of the plaintiff's Constitutional rights.

To appeal Judge Rowe's judgment to the Supreme Court in Pennsylvania would be folly.

CHAPTER XV

"The Letter"

Night after night, following P. J. Rowe's decision, I lay wide-eyed in bed staring at the ceiling in the darkness. I was haunted by my last encounter with Tricia as she hung over the side of her gerichair, trembling, friendless, frightened, not knowing what had happened to her. Just six months before, the charge nurse had said as she assigned me the task of feeding her, "I'll let you feed Tricia. She's a slow eater but she really enjoys her food. I'm sure you'll find this a challenging task."

Now, dinner over in less than 25 minutes, her gerichair had been trundled into "The Dungeon" where I was feeding Hope Knight and where Tricia was to wait for someone to wheel her to her room and put her into bed. Would her teeth be brushed? Was her mouth still sore? Raucous music blared from the tape recorder which had been turned up too high and assaulted her senses for there, trembling, was my old friend, Tricia, dangling over the side of her chair without benefit of a pillow to soften the cutting edge—right hand almost touching the floor. I rose from my chair, crossed over to her to say softly, "Tricia dear, I haven't really forgotten you but the nurse said that I was to feed Hope Knight instead of you." At that moment I knew that Tricia hadn't forgotten me—although I'm sure Mr. Osterhauser would aver that my believing that was just the result of my "subjective" nature—for at the sound of my voice she straightened up in her chair and as I softly stroked her gnarled old hand the bony fingers clutched mine. I could feel tears welling so with a final pat I said that I had to go back to Hope. When I looked again, Tricia was once more draped over the side of her chair—the very picture of despair. No one cared. Her friend had disappeared once more—and this time, Tricia, forever. I told myself that I was glad that Tricia would never know what my trying to help her had cost.

Time and again my thoughts would turn to Osterhauser and the Judges and I felt much as a rape victim must feel. These five "officers of the Court" had censured me. And without benefit of a psychological or psychiatric evaluation, with their outrageous assault on my character and reputation, they had attempted to destroy me. What left the bitter taste was the fact that throughout the whole ordeal I was powerless to fight back. Yes, I was sure I knew how a rape victim must feel although my violation would leave no physical scars nor would I have access to any support group. Certainly they must be elated over their conquest. "It doesn't matter how it's done for the idea is to win, isn't it?" seems to be the theme of most TV legal dramas.

Sometimes the gray dawn would pierce my room before I fell asleep. Or I would doze off hearing the voice of the investigator from the Bureau of Professional and Occupational Affairs after he asked me if the judges had ever talked to me. When I said that they had never even seen me he asked if anyone from Elm Grove had ordered a psychological or psychiatric examination. I assured him that had never been done and then, apologetically he asked, "Virginia, have you ever sought the services of a psychiatrist? I have to ask you this." The question to me was so ludicrous that I laughed and responded forcibly, "Absolutely not!" He said, "I didn't mean to make you angry but I had to ask that." Then he frowned and added, "Do you realize, Virginia, that these men have slandered you?"

"Slandered you! Slandered you!" and I would finally fall asleep.

Night after night, week after week, until I finally felt that the only way I could rid myself of this depressing feeling was to write to the presiding judge of the Court of Appeals. He hadn't given me a chance to defend myself so I would just have to take it. Maybe then I could go to bed and sleep.

His address was obtained from *Pennsylvania Telephone Directory, July 1990* edition and the following letter was sent certified with a return receipt requested. Within the week it was returned to me marked, "Not at this address." Copies of the letter which had been sent to the other two judges of the Court of Appeals must have been delivered for they didn't come back.

Undaunted, I decided to try again. This time I called the chambers of the judge who had told Osterhauser, Elm Grove's attorney, to "Speak up!", and asked how a letter to the judge should be addressed. When the secretary appeared hesitant I added that I had a copy of the *Pennsylvania Telephone Directory* and I knew that the address listed in the directory was incorrect so I thought she might help me. With this she obligingly relayed the address and told me to mark the envelope c/o of the Prothonotary and the judge would be sure to get it. I tucked the first envelope with its green card of affirmation taped to the back into the newly addressed second envelope, went back to the post office, and once again sent my letter with a return receipt requested. This time it had to be delivered for, in my mail box, I found two signed return receipts.

And after mailing that letter I went to bed and slept soundly!

Presiding Judge Rowe
Court of Appeals
Federal Building
9th and Market
Philadelphia, PA 19107

Re: No 8622 Philadelphia 1991
J A 589092
Carl A. Lindstrom and Virginia K. Lindstrom vs Elm Grove, Inc.

Judge Rowe:

For almost three months I have studied the complete record of this case from its presentation to the Court of Common Pleas on 4 April 1991 to your final statement, "Accordingly we affirm the trial court order sustaining appellee's demurrer. Order affirmed.", on 4 August 1992. For almost three months I have debated the idea of writing to you—not that it will restore my character and reputation which you so viciously trashed in your decision—but simply because, in writing, it will make me feel better, and I think for one who, in your words, causes "considerable disturbance" and who finds it "impossible to restrain herself", three months is a sufficiently long time. You see, Sir, I am not the impulsive shrew you have strung up on your gallows to be gaped at by all who read your decision.

During the 200th anniversary of the celebration of our Bill of Rights, in the very cradle of the birth of that great document, I watched the judges in two courts attempt to kill that document. You accused me of being "outraged"—again your word—when in reality I was "determined," but before you are finished reading this letter may you know the difference between "outrage" and "determination"—for this is the voice of "outrage".

I am outraged because a judge was willing to subvert the written facts, to bend the truth, to make it conform to his opinion. I am outraged because a judge, sitting on the bench in the Court of Appeals, should act more like a prosecutor in the hire of the defendant than an equal dispenser of justice. To make my point I must quote from some on your "findings".

Page 6—"The record is equally devoid of the slightest suggestion that appellee has neglected a significant health care or dietary need of any resident." This case, Judge Rowe, was not about the dietary needs of residents. It is obvious to me that although you gleaned from Exhibit C that which would help you in your decision you neglected to read my notes to the dietitian in their entirety and my complaint of April 1991. This case was not about the dietary needs of the residents, but of the patients—specifically the patients whom I had fed—and of my needs if ever I became a patient. I clearly stated in paragraph one of Exhibit C that what the residents did was none of my business.

Much to-do was made of the fact that my leaving Elm Grove was not constructive eviction. You were correct in stating on page 6 that "A Resident's rights are primarily for service"—and with those services went a place to lay my head at night whether in #-113 or Ashley House, or Laurel. But when I discovered that PA Code 28, under which Elm Grove was licensed, meant absolutely nothing to its administrators only an idiot would have remained in such an environment to find herself at a later date alone, incapacitated, with no one allowed to advocate for her. To find herself fed 'mainstream,' her dietary needs irrelevant, and not able to consult with the Community physician because he was a "busy man and his time is money!" Anticipatory? Absolutely! But that is the very reason why the elderly enter Continuing Care Retirement Communities! In anticipation of what might happen to them. That is part of the selling of these Communities.

On Page 9 you lose me completely: "That section is entitled 'Patient Rights' and provides that the governing body of a regulated health care facility is required to establish and adhere to written policies regarding the rights and responsibilities of patients. The record reveals that the appellee has complied with the requirements in that appellee's Resident Guide Book containing a section entitled 'Patient/Resident's Rights' which mirror the rights specified in 201.29." This is complying?!! To print this mandated Code somewhere between how to do the laundry and how to take care of the trash? The Code says, "The facility shall post in a conspicuous place near the entrance on each floor a notice which sets forth the policy intent of 201.29 relating to patients rights." Printing the policy in a collection of "mundane things" (the Court's term) cannot be construed, even in Pennsylvania's courts, as "posting in a conspicuous place"!

"Not a slightest suggestion that the appellee has neglected a significant health care of any patient?" Why the record is replete with such violations. How about, "Medication. . .shall be administered by the same licensed person who prepared the dose for administration. . ." (Nurses aides are not authorized to give any medication—and I'm certain volunteers would fall into this category) 211.9.c. Read again paragraph two of my notes to the dietitian.

"Food shall be prepared to meet individual needs." 211.6.f.

"The consistency of the food should be modified (cut, chopped, pureed or ground) to meet the needs of the individual patient" 211.6.f.

How is Elm Grove's "mainstream" rubbish consistent with these requirements?

"Nurses notes shall be written and signed. . .not limited to, observations made concerning the general condition of the patient. . ." 211.5.0.4.

Why, in the care of my old friend, Tricia, hadn't a nurse or an aide discovered Tricia's need for dental surgery? Why was this left to a volunteer who just two days before had been told to keep her mouth shut—no observations nor criticisms would be countenanced? I don't think it is necessary to belabor the point further. I submit, Judge Rowe, you saw in my notes and in my complaint only what you wanted to see!

I never—repeat never—caused a "considerable disturbance" (your charge, page 9) in my eight months of volunteer work in Ashley House. Three times I offered an observation to the nurses as I fed Tricia, Nellie and others. But PA Code 28.211.12 says, "Nursing personnel shall be aware of the nutritional needs and fluid intake of patients and assist promptly where necessary in the feeding of patients. A procedure shall be established to inform the dietetic service of. . .patient's dietetic problems. Food and fluid intake of patients shall be observed, and observations from normal shall be recorded and reported to the charge nurse and the physician." That was exactly what I did—reported my observations to Drusilla, Bertha, Merrie, nurses on duty. I offered my observations, simply and quietly, and three times I got the very same response, "I'll put it in the record but the kitchen doesn't pay any attention to us." And after a third same reaction I asked if I could run interference for Tricia and was told, "Absolutely! Go to the Dietitian."

Hence my "notes" (Exhibit C) for which I offer no apology. I was determined to help my old friend as well as the nurses to whom the kitchen "paid no attention." I'm sorry you weren't able to distinguish between "determination" and "outrage." I was determined to go through channels to find the person responsible for making the kitchen respond to the requests of the nurses and thereby help Tricia, Nellie, and others. If my quest led all the way to Near and he was reluctant to make the kitchen shape up I was willing to go to State and Federal regulatory agencies. I quote PA Code 28. 211.11(e) ". . .Goals of the care plan shall be set. . .to maintain the present level of functioning of the patients".

The disregard of all of the above edicts of PA Code 28 by the Courts is a sad commentary on judicial review but I think, in your decision, what I resent the most is your characterization of Near and Sharpe as caring administrators who gave me a second chance to stop being disruptive, and your depicting me as a shrew who couldn't control myself! When, just two nights after Near's edict that I could feed Tricia and Nellie so long as I offered no opinions or criticisms, I discovered Tricia was in great pain, are you so pusillanimous that you would have crept silently to your apartment and let this 90-year-old suffer? I'm afraid, Judge Rowe, I was reared in a Christian home where I was taught that I am my brother's keeper. I caused no commotion—and I would defy the nurse to say I did—as I called Tricia's problem to her attention. I knew from her expression that she resented my observation, but she said, "Well, I'll put in the report that Tricia should see the dentist." And I knew two days later, when a second nurse said softly to me, "Tricia saw the dentist today," that my name, had to have been in the report for Bertha to know that I had reported Tricia's problem. And I am not sorry I wrote my memo to the dietitian about Tricia's supper that night. Belle had asked me to report to her anything I thought needed her attention at our meeting of September 20. I have debated long and hard your reason for writing on page 4 that "appellant wife objected to the fact that the food on the patient's tray was fibrous and needed to be cut for the patient to swallow it". My old friend, Tricia, was blind and couldn't cut her food. For seven months I had "cut" it for her. The memo to the dietitian decried the fact that I had to chop finely (mince)—surely you know the difference between just cutting food and chopping fine or mincing—two gummy noodles and two tough meat balls which was all this poor old patient could eat in just over an hour. And I couldn't feed her the poorly cooked and fibrous peas because she choked. How does one cut a pea, I wonder.

I'm glad that my husband and I attended the oral argument— if it could be called an "argument"—before the Court of Appeals. I put the word, "argument" in quotation marks for having taught speech in Pittsburgh years ago I can declare Jack F. Osterhauser's mumbled performance that morning absolutely pathetic from his inaudible beginning when he was told to speak up to his conclusion in less than three minutes. Had we not attended this "argument" we would have thought that comments in your judgment such as "despite the considerable disturbance her complaints caused the staff" had been presented to you orally. But Anderson Jonz has assured us that your decision is based solely on the court records plus that one argument to which Mr. Jonz was not even allowed a rebuttal.

All I can say is, "How sad—how sad that I should have lived so long as to encounter a man willing to slander me, to make it impossible for me ever to enter another retirement Community!" For, as we told Mr. Jonz in January 1991 when Elm Grove offered us $112,889 to go away but the offer carried with it this statement, "It is not our desire to have them (Lindstroms) stay and continue to engage in confrontational behavior which is disruptive to the smooth operation of our facility", that Elm Grove would have to add a letter of apology to its offer for we had never engaged in confrontational behavior disruptive to the facility. This was Near's method of striking out at us only after we had declared our intention of leaving the Community. No retirement Community would ever open its doors to people who are confrontational and disruptive to the Community. And likewise, no one would ever be receptive to a woman who causes considerable disturbances and who cannot control herself when she is outraged. Yes, Judge Rowe, you have sealed my future. If your purpose was to punish me for attempting to bring to court the behavior of Elm Grove's administration then you have been even more successful than Near and Sharpe combined.

Some 60 years ago I was made to memorize in English class these lines:

> "Who steals my purse steals trash,
> 'Tis something, nothing.
> 'Twas mine, 'tis his, and has been slave to thousands.
> But he who filches from me my good name
> Robs me of that which not enriches him
> And makes me poor indeed."

Elm Grove got my purse: Presiding Judge Rowe stole my good name.

Sincerely,
Virginia K. Lindstrom
(Mrs. Carl A. Lindstrom)

Copies: Two other Appellate Judges

POSTSCRIPT

Following the disposition of Carl's and my case on August 27, 1991 by the Court of Common Pleas, Carl and I felt that common law now could seal the fate of those entering a Continuing Care Retirement Community—that any administrator, with impunity, could abuse his position if he were so inclined in spite of previously passed legislation. For, in his decision, Judge Warren Mark had agreed with Elm Grove's attorney that state and federal legislation for the protection of patients in health care facilities of Continuing Care Retirement Communities cannot be implied to include independent-residents in the Community; that the written policies of the Board of Directors of a Continuing Care Retirement Community are in place solely for the patients in the Community's care facility; that unless a person is some sort of guardian for the patient he has no right to advocate for the patient; and unless the patient is a co-plaintiff in a law suit the plaintiff has no cause to bring complaints of the patients' mistreatment to court.

So, as we appealed our case to a higher court, Carl and I explored the health care regulatory agencies in the Commonwealth of Pennsylvania to determine if there were a statutory recourse for complainants who charge administrators of Continuing Care Retirement Communities with abuse of elderly, helpless patients in their care facilities. We found none: there is no regulatory authority over Continuing Care Retirement Communities and their administrators in their management of a continuum of care; no governmental licensure of Continuing Care Retirement Community administrators and no standard of ethics or oversight of their conduct.

From the Pennsylvania Departments of Health and State we were informed that:

"The retirement community as a residential setting is not regulated as it is considered independent living."

/s/ Andrew Major, Director, Bureau of
Quality Assurance, Pennsylvania
Department of Health.

"Neither the Board, nor the Bureau has any regulatory authority with respect to continuing care retirement communities and the individuals who administer those communities."

/s/ George L. Shevlin, Commissioner,
Bureau of Professional and Occupational
Affairs, Department of State,
Commonwealth of Pennsylvania.

". . . I must advise you that the State Board of Examiners of Nursing Home Administrators has no statutory authority to regulate administrators of continuing care retirement communities, even those which provide a continuum of care. To my knowledge. . . there is no administrative agency with such authority. . . ."

/s/ Suzanne Rauer, Prosecuting Attorney,
Bureau of Professional and Occupational
Affairs, Department of State,
Commonwealth of Pennsylvania.

". . . an administrator of a continuing care retirement community is not required a nursing home administrator's license."

> /s/ Susan Ott, State Board of Examiners
> of Nursing Home Administrators,
> Bureau of Professional and Occupational
> Affairs, Department of State,
> Commonwealth of Pennsylvania

And, from the Pennsylvania Department of Aging came:

"I have reviewed both the Continuing Care Provider Registration and Disclosure Act and its implementing regulations. I can find only one reference to the qualifications of the manager of the facility that being 3207 (a)(3)(iii)."

> /s/ Carol H. Lyons, Aging Service Specialist
> Pennsylvania Department of Aging

And the above reference states:

"The disclosure statement shall contain a description of the business experience of the proposed manager, if any, in the operation of management of similar facilities."
[40PS 3207 (a)(3)(iii)]

In summation, no health care regulatory agency in the Commonwealth of Pennsylvania has authority to interfere with the administration of a Continuing Care Retirement Community, nor with the conduct nor ethics of administrators thereof, even of those who, in such capacity, direct the health care components of the Community as a whole, including its residential setting. Their conduct is untouchable by any state regulatory agency.

Carl and I also studied the Continuing Care Provider Registration and Disclosure Act (40PS) under which the Pennsylvania Department of Insurance grants Continuing Care Retirement Communities a Certificate of Authority to engage in the business of continuing care. Provisions of this Act, which was passed in 1984, mandate that, with the Certificate, the Continuing Care Retirement Community must comply with all statutes of the Commonwealth, and that both independent-residents and patients in its care facilities are equal—that everyone residing in the Community must be afforded the same rights, privileges, and care. However, the Department of Insurance adamantly disclaims any responsibility for the protection of the rights of any resident in a Continuing Care Retirement Community as well as any regulatory authority to discipline administrators who abrogate those rights. To the Department of Insurance, its purview is solely an oversight of the financial solvency of Continuing Care Retirement Communities as mandated by the Act and none other—it will not enforce any provision of the Act which protects the rights of any resident therein, whether the resident be of an independent status or a health-care patient.

The Department of Insurance, however, in its implementation of the Act mandates a Continuing Care Retirement Community to provide a disclosure statement to prospective residents setting forth the Community's governance, administration, finances, resident-life, and health care within the Department's guidelines. In each disclosure it requires a conspicuous disclaimer so that every prospective resident will be aware that:

> "Issuance of a Certificate of Authority does not constitute approval, recommendation, or endorsement of the facility by the Pennsylvania Insurance Department, nor is it evidence of, nor does it attest to, the accuracy or completeness of the information set out in the disclosure statement."

With such a disclaimer the Department of Insurance severs itself from administrators of Continuing Care Retirement Communities in the Commonwealth of Pennsylvania who may usurp for themselves dominant control over the destiny, rights, and welfare of their elderly residents. What is disclosed by the Community may, or may not, be what the resident receives, and to the Department of Insurance it is immaterial.

At the Office of the Governor, Carl and I were told that we, as individuals, could not bring complaints to any regulatory agency—that such material must be presented by our attorney. Knowing that this was misinformation, and feeling that we had been brushed off, we left without argument to pursue our investigation.

We filed complaints with the Judicial Inquiry and Review Board, and with the Pennsylvania Bar Association, charging unethical conduct of the judiciary and Elm Grove's defendant-attorney who, without substantiation and benefit of due process, had arbitrarily accused me of idiosyncrasies and imagining all my grievances of abuse of my charges, and of being an undisciplined volunteer and a shrew in Elm Grove.

The Judicial Inquiry and Review Board held that such was not in violation of their standards of ethics—that such was but legal error. And the Pennsylvania Bar Association wrote:

> "Please be advised that it is the charge of the Pennsylvania Bar Association Ethics Committee to respond to attorneys' inquiries and to lend assistance to attorneys based upon their inquiry of ethical considerations. Our Committee does not respond to anyone who is not a member of the Pennsylvania Bar Association.
>
> Although I appreciate your problem as outlined in your letter, your inquiry is misdirected to the Committee."

Undaunted, Carl and I explored some of the organizations which advocate for the betterment of treatment of elderly, helpless patients in care facilities, and we sent letters to some bureaucracies in the federal government. We appealed to the American Association of Retired Persons, National Senior Citizens Law Center, United States Senate Subcommittee on Aging, National Citizens Coalition for Nursing Home Reform, the United States Department of Health and Human Services, and U.S. Health Care Financing Administration.

Most of the replies which we received can be encapsulated in the one from the National Citizens Coalition for Nursing Home Reform, ". . .we don't know about life care. . . ." But Senator George Mitchell, father of the Nursing Home Reform Amendments of the Omnibus Budget Reconciliation Act, would keep our thoughts in mind in event legislation is proposed to protect independent-residents in Continuing Care Retirement Communities. And Senator Wofford's reply consisted of a copy of Hillary Clinton's "Major Elements of Comprehensive Health Care Reform".

In our search for other umbrellas which may protect the rights, well-being and welfare of all those individuals residing in Continuing Care Retirement Communities, whether independent-residents or patients therein, Carl and I focused on the Continuing Care Accreditation Commission. Elm Grove had been accredited by this Commission and its emphasis on "Quality of Life—Quality of Care" had been of great importance to us.

The Continuing Care Accreditation Commission (CCAC) is an independent organization sponsored by the American Association of Homes for the Aging. This organization accredits Continuing Care Retirement Communities which apply for accreditation and which meet the Commission's standards of governance, administration, finance, resident-life and health care. Elm Grove had extolled its accreditation in attempting to persuade Carl and me, as prospective residents, "to come live with us", had displayed the unique seal of the Accreditation Commission in all of its media advertisements, in its brochures, on the walls of its offices, and on all of its stationary; and lauded its accreditation in self-approbation. But obscured in silence was the fact that the Commission is not a governmental regulatory agency; that a Continuing Care Retirement Community accreditation by the Commission is not mandatory under any law; that a Community voluntarily applies to the Commission for accreditation, pays an application fee, an accreditation fee if accredited, and an annual membership fee thereafter; that re-accreditation occurs only once in every five years; and that a Community which does not opt for accreditation by the Commission is not necessarily sub-standard and hence not worthy of consideration.

Heed the warning of the Accreditation Commission printed in its brochure which is presently being distributed and made available to the Public:

"Neither the American Association of Homes for the Aging nor the Continuing Care Accreditation Commission is connected with or responsible for the Administration's acts, personnel, property, or practices of Accredited facilities, nor does AAHA or CCAC warrant an accredited facility's compliance with the CCAC standards."

Finally, after months of frustration, in our determination to find a receptive audience we arrived at the Office of the Attorney General. Mr. Preate, Pennsylvania's Attorney General, asked Daniel Clearfield, Executive Deputy Attorney General of his Public Protection Division to arrange to meet with us. After listening to our complaint Mr. Clearfield offered this kindly advice:

> "Judges know that attorneys will do and say anything to defend their clients; so, Mrs. Lindstrom, you'll just have to accept the judgment of P. J. Rowe. We can't change it."

Additionally, he postured that the only resolution of our case would be the enactment of legislation that would provide a recourse to independent-residents in Continuing Care Retirement Communities in the future. Complaints to the Attorney General of Continuing Care Retirement Communities engaging in deceptive representations to induce prospective residents to enter into contract for life care, of misrepresenting services and care provided, and failing to comply with guarantees and warranties given to residents prior to, or after contract, have no recourse within his office under Pennsylvania Unfair Trade Practices and Consumer Protection Law, 73 PS, of which he is custodian.

We left Mr. Clearfield a somewhat voluminous history, with documented supporting correspondence and court records of our confrontation with Elm Grove. We hoped through this he might recognize the rights of elderly helpless patients in Continuing Care Retirement Communities to advocacy on their behalf by anyone who observes their abuse, and to recognize the rights of independent-residents who, as volunteers, may advocate for the betterment of such individuals without being decreed idiosyncratic, a shrew, and as one who is "unable to adjust to Community-life" and "disruptive to the smooth operation of the Community" for so doing.

Months later, on February 24, 1994, came correspondence from Mr. Clearfield:

> "For the record the Attorney General's Office does not have authority to enforce the Continuing Care Providers Act, even if

there were something in that Act that Elm Grove violated in their deplorable treatment that you received.

You have done everything of which I am aware to pursue your claim against Elm Grove. Even though your civil suit was unsuccessful, you, at least, had the opportunity to attempt to vindicate your rights. It seems that situations such as yours, which have prompted real effort to reform present laws and to protect older Pennsylvanians would be wonderful vindication of your position."

To Mr. Clearfield I say, "Thank you! Thank you sincerely for agreeing with me that what I had experienced at the hands of Elm Grove's administrators was deplorable treatment." But in addition to thank you I must say to Mr. Clearfield that until—and not until—real efforts are forthcoming to reform present laws to protect older Pennsylvanians will I be truly vindicated. Not until someone in the Commonwealth of Pennsylvania reads and implements the entire Continuing Care Provider Registration and Disclosure Act which the General Assembly passed in 1984—be it the Insurance Department, the Health Department, the Department of Aging, or the Attorney General's Office. If the Attorney General does not have the authority to enforce that Act then insist on legislation for such authority. The General Assembly's time and tax payers' dollars went into passing that law. Its intent and spirit should not be dismissed. It should not languish on the shelf collecting dust just because no one, no department, has the authority to enforce it in its entirety.

So, until someone or some office can enforce this law we make several recommendations to any elderly citizen contemplating a move to a Continuing Care Retirement Community. First, anyone seeking admission to any Continuing Care Retirement Community must insist on a clause in the agreement or an addendum that will assure him, at the independent living level of care, the same protection provided to residents in its care facilities under Pennsylvania statutes. The Continuing Care Provider Registration and Disclosure Act assures it. Insist on it in the agreement.

Next, before you succumb to glossy pamphlets, to tapes which assure you that an Elm Grove "allows you to be you", and to an admissions director's dire warning that "when you need it, it's too late", go home, dust off your Bible and read again the story of Jacob and Esau as found in Genesis 25, verses 29 to 34, and then ask yourself if you're really willing to sell your birthright for a mess of pottage.

And last, heed St. Paul's warning to the Hebrews in which he writes, "Faith is the confidence of things hoped for, the evidence of things unseen." For without protective legislation you will enter a Continuing Care Retirement Community solely on faith and trust. Faith and trust are all you have. Faith and trust are all there is.